This Is What Readers Are Saying About This Publication.

Take your croissant work to the next level. I'm carrying this book wherever I go and savouring every page. The science is well explained, as are the many other details. As a Paris trained pastry chef, I'm learning even more on this subject from Jimmy's book. I don't think it's too hard for a beginning baker. Thank you for publishing this gem, sure to become a classic must-have read.

French bakery 5.0 out of 5 stars on Amazon.com, *Sure to become a must-have reference*

I just bought this book, and I have to say it's fantastic. Chef and Author Jimmy Griffin is an amazing person who is gifted in teaching the art of viennoiserie. He explains the different folding techniques used in each process and clearly explains the resulting eating qualities from using the various folds. He has numerous videos uploaded to YouTube, which help explain his methods. I have never met the man, but I have followed him on Instagram for years. I have to say, I am in awe of him. Not only did he once got attacked by a conger eel, but he also broke his back. His resilience and passion for his craft are evident in his book. I have taken lamination courses from Chef Peter Yuen, Chef Hans Ovando and other chefs throughout the years. Chef Griffin's book is just as incredible as their courses. I highly recommend buying his book. I am looking forward to the printed copy once it comes in. You should also follow him on Instagram @jimmyg51.

247 baker, 5.0 out of 5 stars on Amazon.com, *Incredible book on lamination*

I'm a young pastry cook who works with lamination on a daily basis. This book is an amazing supplement to what I've learned from my head pastry chef at work. Between Jimmy's explanations of the technical side of lamination to the recipes that he shares with his readers to the detailed descriptions of the various pastries he's made; this is probably the best book anyone could buy on lamination

James Newman 5.0 out of 5 stars Amazon.com, *Amazing book for Debutantes and cooks of all levels.*

Sold already in 82 countries/regions globally. Available in three formats
1. eBook
2. Paperback
3. Hardcover

Copyright © 2024 by Jimmy Griffin All rights reserved. No part of this book may be reproduced, transmitted, or stored digitally or otherwise, in any manner, including photocopying, recording, and imaging without written permission of Barna Caf Ltd. Publications. For permission to reprint material, contact Jimmy Griffin at griffjimmy@gmail.com.

Additional Copyright © 2024 ; No AI Training Permitted: Without in any way limiting the author's [and publisher's] exclusive rights under copyright, any use of this publication to "train" generative artificial intelligence (AI) technologies to generate text is expressly prohibited. The author reserves all rights to license uses of this work for generative AI training and development of machine learning language models.

When quoting material under Fair Use exemptions, please use the following citation:

Griffin, J. (2020). *The Art of Lamination. Advanced Technical Laminated Pastry Production 2020.* (2nd ed.). Barna Caf Enterprises Ltd.

Published by
Barna Caf Enterprises Ltd.
Wild Winds, Forramoyle West
Barna, Co Galway
Ireland. H91 XHY7

Website: http://jimmyg.ie
YouTube: http://www.youtube.com/c/JimmyGriffinbaking/
Instagram: @jimmyg51
FaceBook Page: https://www.facebook.com/groups/theartoflamination/

First edition June 2020

Revised XL edition April 2024

ISBN - 978-1-0686508-0-2

Table of Contents

Table of Contents 2

Table of Tables 6

Glossary Of Terms and Abbreviations 6

Foreword 7

Dedications 8

Influences in My Professional Life 8

Section 1 Knowledge and Lessons #1-4 11

Abstract 12

Anatomy of a Croissant 14

Overview and Hacks for Laminated Pastry Making 15

The 20 Stages of Laminated Pastry Production and Handling 16

Yeasts Used in Laminated Pastry Making 17

Types of Flour Used in Artisan Baking in America And Europe 18

A Guide to Flour Comparison Worldwide 19

Ingredient Choices Used in Great Pastry Making 21

Other Ingredients in The Pastry 21

Desired Dough Temperature 26

Understanding the Dough 27

Maintaining A Sourdough Starter 29

Recipe for Starter Refresh Example 30

Process of Preparation 33

Important Liquid Sourdough Makeup Points 34

Proofing Pastry in The Home 35

Baking Using Different Oven Types 37

The Bakers' Percentage Explained 40

Core Temperature and Chilling Pastry Using Ice Blankets 42

Understanding Core Temperature in Proofing Pastry 45

Recipes Used in This Publication 46

Processing Factors 47

How To Prepare A Butter Block On YouTube 48

- Lock-In and Lamination Numbering System 48
- Dough Touching Points 49
- Steps And Stages of Preparing Fermented Laminated Pastry 50
- Production of Laminated Croissant Pastry – Sample Recipe 51
- Lesson #1 the 3-4-3 system 53
- The Lock-In 3 53
- The 4-Fold or Book Turn 55
- The 3-Fold 56
- Pastry Sheeter Settings 57
- Pre-Lock-In 3-4-3 Pastry Height Discussion 57
- Lock-In and First 4-Fold Sheeting Settings Overview 58
- The 3- Fold Sheeting Settings 59
- Final Sheeting Settings 3-4-3 59
- Cutting The Belly Of The Pastry to Ease Elastic Recoil 60
- Lesson #2 The 5-4-3 System 61
- The 5 Lock-In 61
- The 4-Fold 62
- Layer Calculation Example After Subtraction Of DTP 4-Fold 64
- The 3-Fold 64
- Lesson #3 The 3-4-4 System 65
- The Lock-in 3 66
- The 1st 4-fold 66
- The 2nd and Final Fold In The 3-4-4 System 67
- Lesson #4 the 3-3-3 / 3 system 68
- The Lock-In 3 69
- Overview of the 3-3-3-3 System, Lock-In, Sheeting and First Trifold 71
- Processing Notes Recap for The Lamination 3-3-3 / -3 72
- Keeping Count of The Number of Folds Made on The Pastry 73
- Recommended Layering for Different Pastry Sizes/Weight 73
- Processing the Pastry - Rolling Out the Croissants 73
- Croissant and Chocolatine Cutting Guide Table 74

Egg Washing and Proofing 75

Baking Temperature Factors 76

After Baking - Care of Pastry 77

Section 2 Recipes and Techniques 78

1. The Almond Twice-Baked Croissant 78
2. Almond Cream Recipe 79
3. Rum Syrup Recipe 79
4. Twin Lamination Croissant and Chocolate Croissant Pastry 79
5. Preparing Chocolate Flavoured Butter for Twin Lamination 81
6. Base Recipes for Croissant Pastry Production 81
7. Twin Lamination Pastry with Spelt or Strong Flour 81
8. The Double Chocolate Chocolatine 88
9. Bicolor Croissants and Pain Au Chocolat 3-4-4 89
10. The Orange Chocolate Bicolor Chocolatine 5-4-3 91
11. The Cross-Laminated Croissant and Chocolatine 92
12. The Orange Chocolate Twin Laminated Chocolatine 95
13. The Lye Dipped Croissant 3-3-3 96
14. Four Colour Cross Lamination-The Christmas Chocolatine 98
15. Seaweed Croissant 101
16. Woodgrain Effect Croissant 3-4-3 103
17. Frozen Pre-Proofed Croissants and Viennoiserie 104
18. Making Croissants and Viennoiserie Using Sourdough 106
19. Sweet Puff Paste 3-4-4 / 4 107
20. Savoury Puff Paste Recipe 3-4-4 / 4 111
21. Extra Flaky Puff Paste 3-3-3 / 3-3 112
22. Puff Paste Quiche with Cheese and Onion 113
23. Laminated Brioche 115
24. Kouign Amann 3-4-4 117
25. World Silver Medal 2019 Coupe du Monde Chocolatine 3-4-4 121
26. Raspberry Pear Marinade 3-4-3 126
27. The Crème Pâtissière Recipe 414 g 127
28. Chocolate Pear Baskets 3-4-3 131
29. Pain Aux Raisins 3-4-3 133

30. Cinnamon Swirls 3-4-3 135

31. Apple Pistachio/Apple Raspberry 137

32. Cappuccino Chocolatine - Three Types of Pastry 138

33. Raspberry/Strawberry Chocolatine 139

34. Strawberry Shortcake 139

35. Nutella/Coffee 140

36. Raspberry Brioche Sablée 141

37. Strawberry Chocolate Twist 142

38. Nutella Cruffin Style Pastry 143

Appendix - A – Materials and Methods 145

Materials and Methods 146

The Equipment, Small Tools and Other Items Required In The Pastry Kitchen 147

Ingredient Storage 153

Weighing Station 153

Mixing Station 153

Dough Storage Containers 154

Lamination Station 154

Makeup Table and Small Tools 154

Trollies and Baking Trays 155

Freezing Equipment 155

Packaging Station for Sales and Distribution 155

Ingredients and Contact Details 156

Materials and Methods 156

Appendix - B – Pre Fermented Croissant Dough Hand Lamination 164

39. Hand Laminated Croissant 50 % Preferment & Sourdough Levain 165

Other Online Resources 168

Puff Pastry Hand Lamination Bible 169

Christmas Mince Pies made with Butter Puff Pastry 169

Hand rolling a croissant 169

References 170

The Art of Lamination Index 174

Table of Tables

Table 1: Flour types comparison table (Doves Farm, 2020) 20

Table 2: Flour types, ash and protein content (Weekendbakery.com, 2020) 20

Glossary Of Terms and Abbreviations

Beurrage	Preparation/plasticising butter prior to lamination
CDM	Coupe du Monde de la Boulangerie – World Cup of Bakery
CDMC	Coupe du Monde Chocolatine – World Cup of Chocolatine
Core temperature	The temperature at the centre or core of a pastry/block of pastry
DDT	Desired Dough Temperature
DTP	Dough Touching Points
IR	Infrared thermometer
Lamination number	A number given to the number of folds given to the pastry
Lock-in	Placing butter between layers of dough to begin the lamination process
RH	Relative Humidity
RT	Room Temperature
Sheeting	Rolling pastry out thin to fold or cut
WT	Water Temperature

Foreword

Making high quality laminated yeasted pastry requires many capabilities: knowledge, skill, understanding, technical ability, procedure, precision, patience and practice, among other things. Passion is the greatest of all of these. The reward for producing excellent pastry is the satisfaction it brings to its creator and the consumers who delight in this creation time and time again. I hope to stimulate your creativity with the photos and techniques in my book, to give you lots of ideas to create, to imagine and the knowledge to execute these ideas for your own creations.

Jimmy Griffin, President, Coupe Du Monde de la Boulangerie/World Cup of Baking, Paris 2016.

Dedications

I dedicate this book to my beloved family, my wife Bogna, son Dillon and daughters Janice and Sophie. I love you all very much, and I could not have finished this book without your support. 2020 saw a terrible disease, Covid-19, sweep across the world, changing the lives of many millions of people. Many mourners have been left behind. It was also the year that my friend, colleague and mentor at Technological University Dublin, Diarmuid Murphy, parted this world and left us for another, hopefully, brighter place. Diarmuid was one of my lecturers when I studied for my MSc. He brought joy, brightness, humour and interest to all his classes. He was a significant inspiration in my life, prompting me in my appreciation, writing, reading and research in bakery. Diarmuid also loved my croissants and pastry. This book is for you, Diarmuid.

Influences in My Professional Life

There are so many people to who I am thankful to, and I would have to write another book to mention them all. I wish to thank my global bakery family, whose friendships have endured and their influences on me through creativity and passion. Derek O' Brien, my friend and mentor, retired Head of the National Bakery School Kevin Street, Dublin; retired Head of Diploma in German Baking course at Akademie Deutsches Bäckerhandwerk Weinheim, Germany and Director of the Baking Academy of Ireland, Dublin. Over the years, my former Irish bakery team colleagues: Tommy, Frank, Paul, Gemma, Robert, Michelle and Dolores. Dr Frank Cullen has always fully supported me in my work at TU Dublin as a lecturer and inspired me to write and think academically. Finally, my dear friend Christian Vabret, creator of Coupe du Monde de la Boulangerie, has believed in me and honoured me with my appointment of being a juror at world events for nearly two decades. Christian made it possible for me to meet, watch, observe and learn from the world's best bakers. Finally, special thanks to Kathryn Gordon of ICE, NY, Dr Ted Lynch, and Allen Cohn for their proofreading and advice assistance. Many thanks to you all.

About the Author

James, or Jimmy Griffin as he is more popularly known, is a sixth-generation master baker from Galway, Ireland. He has forty years' experience in the bakery industry, growing up in the family business. Jimmy is a specialist in viennoiserie, sourdough, bread and cake production. He holds a Masters' degree in Food Product Development and Culinary Innovation and lectures to honours degree bakery students at the School of Culinary Arts and Food Technology, Technological University, Cathal Brugha Street, Dublin. He also works as an advisor and consultant to industry. Jimmy grew up being competitive and, as an apprentice, won many national bakery competitions. Later in his career, he represented Ireland and competed in the European Championships as the viennoiserie candidate three times, winning bronze at the Coupe D' Europe de la Boulangerie 1997. He went on to coach the very successful Irish bakery team from 2002 until 2005.

Jimmy has also been an international bakery jury member since 2001 for most of the world championships and world master's competitions, the bakery Olympics of the industry. In 2016, Jimmy was appointed as president of the Jury at the Coupe du Monde de la Boulangerie in Paris. He regularly lectures and teaches overseas and has been involved with baking and competitions on most continents of the world. In 2015, he was also honoured by his Russian colleagues and awarded an Honorary Professorship of Stavropol University in Russia. In May 2019, he came out of competitive retirement to compete in the Coupe du Monde Chocolatine in Toulouse, France, taking the silver medal for his creations in hand-laminated pastry at the event. He is very active on social media platforms and regularly updates his pages with exciting recipes, procedures, and products.

Married to his wife Bogna, Jimmy has three children, Dillon (23), Janice (22) and Sophie (14) (2020). In addition to his test baking passion, Jimmy is a licenced fixed-wing pilot, an aerobatic pilot, seaplane pilot, judo blackbelt instructor, divemaster and a former marathon runner. He enjoys writing; his honours degree dissertation titled "An investigative study into the beneficial use of seaweed in bread and the broader food industry" has been viewed and downloaded over 6000 times. He is currently finishing a book featuring internationally acclaimed bakers' recipes named *The Global Master Bakers Cook Book*, a book with many of Griffin's Favourite recipes, titled *Family Secrets – Part 1 1876-2019* the history of the family bakery titled *Fully Baked*, and another book on Panettone and Levito Madre. Jimmy had two brothers, Mark lives with his family in London and David, formerly in Malta. Sadly, while finishing this publication, David died suddenly aged 57 years. We will always remember him in our hearts and our minds. Sleep in peace, David.

Honorary Professor of Bakery and Pastry Arts,

Stavropol University, Russia 2015

With Janice and Bogna Griffin

©2020 James A. Griffin All rights reserved.

Section 1
Knowledge and Lessons #1-4

This book was written in 2020 during the first Global lockdown when the Covid-19 virus shut down the world and its economy. Many bakers and confectioners out of work, students and university lecturers out of college and chefs sought an alternative to hands-on tuition to re-educate their knowledge and skills. The Art of Lamination was written as an educational reference book organised into two sections. Section 1 includes detailed information about pastry make up and baking that likely will help less experienced bakers successfully navigate the recipes in this book. There are four main lamination lessons in the book. While some readers may find the content repetitive, it is a great teaching method, re-enforcing the learning objectives and the numerical terminology designed to help and assist students of The Art of Lamination in remembering not only the how but the why in making laminated pastry. Section 2 is made up of recipes and the detail required to learn how to make the individual pastries presented in the book. I took the time to scale down the recipes to be made both at home and in commercial bakeries and kitchens as desired.

I use only metric measures in this book—all the recipe ingredients are listed in grams—because they are most exact, and using metric measures also allows recipes to easily be made smaller or be scaled-up for mass production. All baking temperatures in the book are given in degrees Celsius (°C). (You can easily find temperature conversion calculators online.) Additionally, many of the recipes include optimal temperatures need for making consistent dough and pastry.

Each recipe is accompanied by a detailed photograph, method and sequence. A list of online resources from my YouTube channel is presented as an appendix to help you navigate the many diverse and different pastries in this book.

Abstract

Internationally, there are as many terms for the folds and type of folds used when laminating pastry as there are languages. In the USA, they refer to letter fold, envelope, double fold, in Ireland and the UK it is a book fold, a half-fold a single fold, fold-over etc.…Then to add further confusion, pastry can be described as being made by the English method, the French method, blitz method, inverse butter method, Dutch method, German method and the Scotch method! It can all become very baffling, especially when translated into a dozen different languages. However, one common denominator encompasses all this process, and that is a numerical solution to the language barriers. Many of the world's top bakers now communicate lamination techniques by describing the folds as a number instead of a name. My colleague Peter Yuen, a noted world lamination specialist, has also taught this system worldwide. This system is truly international, and, in this paper, I explain in detail the correct use of this numbering system.

Additionally, having reviewed countless textbooks on the subject, my teaching and jury work experience seeks out many of the gaps in viennoiserie's education to white art practitioners. This work provides both a scientific and a straightforward explanation of many of the finer points of producing great laminated pastry.

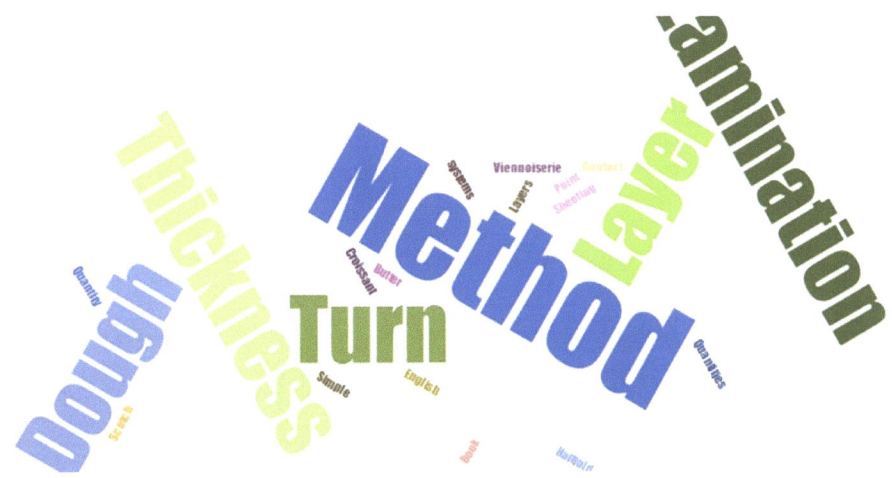

A Brief History of The Croissant from the 17th century

The croissant's birth was a series of evolutionary steps that began with the kipferl form, shared in Austria and Germanic baking at the time, and the invention of flaky, laminated pastry. The first recognised puff pastry recipe or *pâte feuilletée* was documented in François Pierre de la Varenne's 1653 book, *Le Pâtissier François*. This iconic historical cookbook was the first to record recipes and methods of the French pastry arts (Goldstein & Mintz, 2015). According to the Culinary Institute of America (CIA) (2016:289). The croissant was first fashioned by Budapest's Hungarian bakers to signify and celebrate the liberation of their beloved city from the Turkish army in 1686 CIA (2016). However, in *August Zang and the French Croissant*, Chevallier (2009) contradicts this CIA version of events. The Austrian bakers in Vienna were under siege in 1683 by the Turkish invaders who invented the croissant Chevallier (2009:9). The legend recounts that Viennese bakers in 1683, while at work early in the morning, heard the Turkish army digging under Vienna's walls. They alerted their army commanders, and the Turks were routed. The croissant was created to celebrate the liberation of Vienna. Its shape and name were consequent of the crescent moon, a symbol of Turkish tyranny. The French and Italian bakers soon followed after their Viennese counterparts and included this crescent pastry as part of their daily mantra. In its original classical form, the croissant was very different from today's creation as it was made using puff paste with lard and milk, a laminated dough devoid of yeast.

> *When you have mastered puff pastry, you will find it such a satisfying and splendid accomplishment that you will bless yourself for every moment you spent learning the techniques.* Labensky, Sarah, R; Martel, Priscella, Van Damme, Eddy (2009).

Falling sugar prices toward the end of the seventeenth century enabled the rising wealthy merchant dynasties in Vienna and Paris's prosperous cities to trade in sugar, which was once available exclusively to royalty. Café culture, as we know it, was born about this time in Paris. This café culture involved meeting over tea, coffee, and cake to discuss revolutionary ideas against King Louis XIV (Willan, 2016).

Anatomy of a Croissant

Croissants are generally shaped from an isosceles triangle-shaped piece of leavened, laminated pastry and coiled from the base to the tip when forming. They are made using butter or pastry margarine. Croissants are available worldwide in curved, crescent shape or straight. They can be hand made by artisans in bakeries and pastry kitchens or industrially mass-produced, frozen, and distributed across the globe. They are possibly the most globally iconic pastry that conjures up an association with France when seen or spoken about. They are available in different quality standards depending on whether they are laminated with butter, pastry margarine, or other fats. The percentage of laminating butter in a croissant is usually 30% dough weight. The pastry triangle base is referred to as the base or the foot, and the top is known as the tip. The pastry triangle has two flat sides and three cut edges on the outside of the pastry. When a croissant is rolled up, the outsides edges are visible as "steps" or shoulders, and the number of steps is predetermined by the size and length of the isosceles triangles cut to form them. A ratio of 10 cm wide: 30 cm long is common. Additionally, the cut triangle is generally stretched further by the baker's hand, further elongating it and allowing the pastry to have more coils or steps. The croissant should not be stressed too much when forming as it will tear when proofing. When stretched for forming, the pastry should have a graduated thickness extending from the thinnest part at the base to the thickest part at the tip. The bicolor croissant below was made in Reykjavik, Iceland, while assisting Team Iceland as a tutor in January 2018.

Overview and Hacks for Laminated Pastry Making

The laminated pastry is usually made by combining a stiff enriched sweet dough with a sheet or block of butter known as a butter block. The dough and butter should be of roughly the same consistency, which favours the creation of even layer formation when rolled and folded together. While pastry margarine and other hard fats can also be used to achieve lamination, this publication's focus is the production of laminated pastry using butter. The butter should be hammered with a rolling pin, a technique known as *beurrage* in French, to plasticise the butterfat and make it malleable for rolling, and it is then formed into a rectangular block known as a butter block. In the pastry's make-up process, the dough is sheeted out thinly and folded to surround or encapsulate the butter. When the butter and dough combine, it is referred to as pastry.

Standard laminated pastry making practice generally begins with establishing a sandwich of three layers; two layers of dough top and bottom, with the butter block in the centre; like a slice of cheese between two slices of bread. The pastry is formed by rolling or sheeting the dough and butter together in unison. As the pastry is rolled down to form a thin sheet, a process called sheeting, both the dough and butter layers extend out into a thin rectangle of pastry. The dough and butter layers remain separate and intact, forming long thin alternating dough/butter/dough layers in this pastry sheet. Once sheeted to an acceptable thickness, the process of building the number of layers to a desired numerical value is achieved by folding the sheeted pastry into pleats which sit on top of each other like building blocks. The most common folds used in laminated pastry making are a book fold, also known as a 4-fold, and a half fold, known as a 3-fold. Every time the pastry is sheeted, folded, and re-sheeted, additional layers are formed within the pastry. These layers are folded and built up within the pastry, contributing to creating the light eating quality and volume associated with a laminated pastry product. Both the process and temperature control are essential in successful pastry making, as is the number of layers required for a particular product. Croissant generally requires 25 layers; chocolatine 33 layers and puff paste can have well over 145 layers depending on the number of folds given to the pastry.

I have identified 20 separate stages in the processes of producing laminated pastry through different stages, whether baking straight away or freezing/retarding for another day.

The 20 Stages of Laminated Pastry Production and Handling

1. Weighing of the raw materials
2. Mixing times and desired dough temperature 25 °C –26 °C
3. Preparation of the butter block while mixing the dough
4. Bulk fermentation of the dough (45 minutes)
5. Flattening and chilling of the dough (3 °C –4 °C) overnight for cold fermentation
6. Lock-in of the butter into a sandwich between the dough using **3** or **5-**layer lock-in
7. Sheeting #1, reducing the pastry down in thickness to between 3 mm–5 mm and 1st fold
8. Resting in chilled storage (-18 °C between ice blankets if available)
9. Sheeting #2, reducing the pastry down in thickness to between 5 mm –6 mm and 2nd fold
10. Chilling/resting (-18 °C between ice blankets if available)
11. Final sheeting generally to a thickness of between 3.5 mm–4.0 mm
12. Cutting to size and shape
13. Shaping, forming, and traying up
14. Proofing (26 °C –27.5 °C at 80% relative humidity RH) 2 –3 hours, Wobble test, visually observe the separation of layers at the end of proof time
15. Egg washing (recipe page 75)
16. Retardation (3 °C –RH 80%) if holding overnight for baking the following day
17. Freezing (-18 °C) if holding for several days, preferably blast freezing after 3/4 proof
18. Baking – temperature and time which will depend on whether you use a convection or deck oven
19. Cooling on wire racks to prevent the bottoms from becoming soggy
20. Finishing/packing.

Yeasts Used in Laminated Pastry Making

Saccharomyces Cerevisiae, or bakers' yeast as it is commonly known, is the yeast bakers use mostly throughout the world. Yeast comes in many different forms, from fresh to dried and yeast reproduces by a process known as budding. Yeast's reproduction rate ensures that it roughly doubles in quantity every 90 minutes (Berry, *et al.,* 2012). In theory, the quantity of yeast present in a dough can double in 90 minutes, but factors such as dough temperature, enrichment levels, and pH can have a marked effect on yeast reproduction. Placing a yeasted dough into a refrigerator, for example, will slow down yeast reproduction and placing the dough in a warm proofer can accelerate yeast reproduction. There are many types of bakers' yeast available on the market today. Yeast is available as fresh/compressed, freeze-dried/dehydrated and vacuum packed so that the yeast has a very long shelf life at ambient temperature. My personal choice for pastry making is fresh compressed yeast or, if available, osmotolerant fresh yeast, a special yeast sold mainly in Europe to produce brioche and laminated pastry. It performs much better in the high fat/sugar environment of enriched pastry, giving superior tolerance and gassing performance than regular bakers' yeast. Bakers or fresh yeast is the standard stated in all recipes in this book unless otherwise stated. I use 10 g dry/30g compressed yeast, but many people also use 10 g dry to 20 g compressed yeast in smaller batches. Two general types of dried yeast are popular among home bakers today: active dry yeast and instant yeast. It is essential to be aware that active dry yeast needs to be rehydrated, which is dissolved in the dough-making water before mixing into the dough to activate it. Dried yeasts may also contain emulsifiers and bread improvers for use in bread machines, so attention to the ingredient list is wise if baking for people with extreme allergies. Always use warm water to dissolve active yeast and stimulate the yeast back to life. The second type of yeast is instant yeast, and this yeast can be mixed straight into the dough without pre-hydrating. Both types of dried yeasts can be used interchangeably in laminated pastry formulas without recipe adjustment. However, care needs to be taken to rehydrate the active dried yeast if you are using it or suffer poor gassing performance.

In summary, to reinforce the importance of handling yeast correctly, it is best practice to hydrate all yeast forms before making your dough. The warmth of the water encourages good gassing and fermentation of the dough. Always read and follow the manufacturers recommendations when using dry yeast for best results.

Types of Flour Used in Artisan Baking in America And Europe

Calvel's *The Taste of Bread* has an extensive table on page 4 showing protein and ash content of US and French flours (Calvel, 2001). The extraction rate is the quantity of flour extracted from each wheat berry during the milling process. The lower the extraction rate of flour, the whiter the flour will be as the flour is removed from the wheat berry centre, e.g. T-45 flour. The higher the extraction rate, the more bran and percentage of the wheat berry, e.g. T-150 is a dark brown wholemeal flour of almost 98% extraction.

- Type 45: Ash content below 0.50 extraction rate 67% –70%
- Type 55: Ash content 0.50–0.62 extraction rate 75% –78%
- Type 65: Ash content 0.62–0.75 extraction rate 78% –82%
- Type 80: Ash content 0.75–0.90 extraction rate 82% –85%
- Type 110: Ash content 1.00–1.20 extraction rate 85% –90%
- Type 150: Ash content above 1.40 extraction rate 90% –98%

(Calvel, 2001).

Generally, American flour's ash content is measured based on a 14% flour humidity; the ash content numbers cannot be compared directly. For example, a French flour with a measurement of 0.55 ash (type 55) corresponds to a US 0.46 ash content flour. It is also fair to say that there are no direct equivalent flours between the French/German and US types as many US millers do not list flour ash content on the package. A separate flour specification sheet must be requested to establish the ash content of each individual flour type. The inability to establish like-for-like equivalents in flour types is mostly due to the difference in milling process steps by each miller. Milling consists of a series of steps of sorting, grinding, sifting, and regrinding grain. Diverse types of mills process the grain differently; some mills are traditional millstones, while modern mills use steel rollers and all produce variation in the end product. The milling process's goal is gradually extracting the maximum amount of endosperm (the white central part of the grain) while eliminating the bran, which is the roughage on the outside. Each step produces a "stream" of flour (after the sifting process).

The grain undergoing milling can pass through several sets of rollers, each roller descending in thickness as the grain passes through. Each consecutive step in the milling processes removes additional bran from the wheat kernel. The streams or breaks, as they are also called, are separated individually. The first stages of milling produce the weakest flours in terms of protein content. The final step(s) will produce "clear" flours that are very strong and somewhat darker as they contain pieces of the bran. They are mostly considered useful to strengthen doughs where, for example, the percentage of rye flour is high, and therefore the colour is not so critical, such as wholegrain bread. French flours are created by mixing various flour streams to arrive at a predetermined, desired ash content.

Many American mills do not blend individual streams of their flour together but prefer to select blends of flour-based on desired dough properties or strength. Consequently, a direct comparison of the flour's ash content does not guarantee equivalency between types. Higher extraction rates in milling generally imply more of the outer endosperm, a darker flour, and high/greater protein content. Additionally, darker or higher extraction flours have a higher ash content. Non-standardised blending taking place in many mills in America, which creates a scenario whereby a non-standard result in the flour is possible for comparison measures. There is a different system in Germany; generally, it roughly adds a 0 to the French types for the German equivalent compared to French flours. T-55 will become T-550 flour (Weekendbakery.com, 2020).

A Guide to Flour Comparison Worldwide

I have included two tables on page 20, which will help me compare the complex issue of flour types. They are for use as a guide; they are a rough comparison only and are not a like-for-like swap; different milling styles and a different grist or blend of grains give each flour type its diverse character and quality. The first table's information was from the Dove's Farm website, but I added extra content to include other countries, such as Canada and Ireland. Doves Farm offers many great baking resources and makes brilliant flour.

Table 1: **Flour types comparison table (Doves Farm, 2020)**

	Milled from 100% of the grain	Extraction rate 85%	White bread flour	White bread flour	White flour	Very fine flour low extraction
Argentina	½	0	00	-	000	0000
Australia	Wholemeal flour		Bread flour		Plain flour	Cake/pastry flour
Canada	Whole wheat flour		Bread flour	Bakers patent	All-purpose flour	Pastry/cake flour
China	小麦面粉	-	-	-	中筋麵粉	-
Czech Republic	Celozrnná mouka	Hrubá mouka	Polohrubá mouka	-	Hladká mouka	Hladká mouka
France	Farine intègral 150	110	80	65	55	45
Germany	Vollkorn 1600	1050	812	-	550	405
Holland	Volkorenmeel	Gebuilde bloem	Tarwe bloem	-	Patent bloem	Zeeuwse bloem
India	Chakki atta	Atta	-	-	Maida /	-
Ireland	Wholemeal flour	Wheat meal flour	Strong bakers flour	Bakers flour	Soft flour	Pastry/biscuit flour
Italy	Integrale	Tipo 2	Tipo 1	-	0	00
Poland	Razowa	Sitkowa	Chlebowa	-	Luksusowa	Tortowa
Portugal	Harina integrale 150	110	80	70	55	45
Slovakia	Celozrnná mouka	Hrubá mouka	Polohrubá mouka	-	Hladká mouka	Hladká mouka
Spain	Harina integrale 150	110	80	70	55	45
Spain	Harina integrale 150	110	80	70	55	45
Portugal	Harina integrale 150	110	80	70	55	45
UK	Wholemeal flour	Brown flour	Strong bread	-	Plain flour	Patent flour
USA	Whole wheat flour	First clear flour	High-gluten bread flour	-	All-purpose flour	Pastry flour

Table 2: **Flour types, ash and protein content (Weekendbakery.com, 2020)**

Ash content	Protien	USA	German	French	Italian	Netherlands	UK
~0.4%	~9%	Pastry flour	405	45	0	Zeeuwse bloem	Pastry flour
~0.55%	~11%	All-purpose flour	550	55	0	Patentbloem	Bakers flour
~0.8%	~14%	High-gluten flour	812	80	1	Tarwebloem	Strong bakers
~1%	~15%	First clear flour	1050	110	2	Gebuilde bloem	-
>1.5%	~13%	Whole wheat flour	1700	150	Farina integrale	Volkorenmeel	Wholemeal

Ingredient Choices Used in Great Pastry Making

Firstly, the ingredients used should be of the highest possible quality. The flour used for viennoiserie should not be too strong and should exhibit good elasticity. When processed into dough can be made using spelt, all-purpose flour, T-55, T-65, T-45, wholemeal or other special flours such as T-45 Gruau Rouge flour. Gruau Rouge is a low-extraction, very white flour with a lot of elasticity and ideal for viennoiserie. If this cannot be sourced, a baker's bread-making flour combined with a soft pastry type flour in a 75% / 25% or a 70% / 30% ratio will give a very favourable result. Tests using 100% Spelt flour have also produced very satisfactory products. The butter, if possible, should also be a special dry, hardened butter with a fat content of between 84%- –86%.

- The type of yeast stated in all the recipes is fresh, compressed yeast
- If using dried yeast, use 1/3 –1/2 of the weights given in the recipes for fresh yeast
- Use osmotolerant yeast if available for a high-sugar/high-fat environment
- Lower protein flour with extensible gluten characteristics 11.5% –12.8% protein
- A preferment recipe with a minimum of 25% of the flour will greatly assist elasticity and handling (see Appendix B)
- A hardened butter with an 84% –86% butterfat content with good plasticity qualities

Other Ingredients in The Pastry

Water

Hydration of the dough is essential. Many bakers use between 46% –55% hydration for laminated dough so that the dough consistency matches that of the butter for ease of lamination and superior layering. Use filtered water where possible to remove chlorine and other minerals, which may affect and delay fermentation.

Liquid Levain

Will add both extensibility and maturity to the dough, with subtle flavour along with slow leavening, aiding greater volume and extensibility. Levain assists in the development of an open honeycomb internal structure. I use a 1:2:2 liquid levain fermented for at least 6 hours before putting it in the dough for my croissant dough.

Yeast

Fresh osmotolerant yeast is used by pastry chefs and bakers for high-sugar/high-fat doughs, assisting in more outstanding controlled fermentation. The gassing of the yeast gives stability in the fermentation of the dough. It also adds to the lightness or airiness of the pastry.

Sugar

Sugar acts as a sweetener to the dough and as a portion of food for the yeast. The sugar also improves the colour of the baking pastry, giving it a golden colour.

Salt

Salt gives flavour to the dough; it also has an essential function of controlling the yeast's fermentation and adding colour pigmentation to the pastry. Use organic natural salt where possible. I use organic Oriel sea salt as a natural salt, free of anti-caking agents and additives.

Malt Powder or Liquid

Malt is not only good food for yeast development and stability, but it also gives the baked pastry a classic chestnut brown colour on the crust. Non-active malt should be used. Honey/glucose are good substitutes if you cannot access malt; it can also be left out of the recipe if required.

Butter Used in The Dough

Adding butter into the dough gives the pastry a nicer eating quality. The butterfat acts as a lubricant to the dough's gluten, thereby improving its extensibility in mixing, lamination, proofing and baking.

Pâté Fermentée

Like liquid levain, pâté fermentée tends to add a more pronounced flavour to the dough and assists in the pastry's elasticity and rolling. It also contributes to an open honeycomb structure internally.

Lamination Butter Used During Coupe Du Monde Chocolatine (CDMC) - Lescure

Beautiful Lescure hardened butter is specially made for excellent flavour and quality laminated viennoiserie production. The higher fat content/lower moisture content enables the dough to form beautiful layers easier. The butter also has a higher melting point which helps keep the delicious flaky layers intact together throughout the process of production.

Chocolate Sticks Valrhona Used During CDMC

The chocolate sticks were provided for the Chocolatine World Cup by the globally famous Valrhona chocolate brand. Valrhona chocolate bars are specially made for baking and do not burn in the oven of premium quality.

Egg Wash

Egg wash is the varnish on the pastry. Not only does it give a beautiful shine and colour, but it also adds flavour, and it helps the layers at the top of the chocolatine to stick together and not fly off the top when baking. See egg wash recipe page 75.

Understanding The Butter

Butter is an emulsion of oil and water made from dairy cream. Butter comes in many forms, including salted, unsalted, country butter, clarified butter, ghee, spreadable butter, fractionated butter, recombined butter and dry butter, to name but a few. The texture achieved by butter is a result of the degree of processing given the butter during the manufacturing process. Like chocolate, the fat in butter undergoes a tempering factor that establishes a crystalline network, which results in the smooth texture which butter exhibits as raw material and a portion of food. Salt is added for both flavour and to extend the shelf life of the butter. Butter has many applications and functions in laminated pastry making. In the croissant dough, which is made before lamination, regular soft butter is added as an enriching agent. It also contributes to a shortening effect in the finished product by lubricating the mixed dough's gluten. I do not recommend using home-made butter for lamination as it is too soft, has too much water and too little butterfat. A harder, dry butter is, therefore, used for the lamination process. This hard, dry butter is made from fermented cream and has had some of the liquid components removed to add more hard fat in its place. Plasticity and high melting point are the properties bakers seek in this type of butter. If the butter is too hard and lacks plasticity, the butter will fracture in the lamination process leading to uneven distribution and layer formation. Butter is typically made up of the following components:

- Butterfat   80.0% –83.0 %
- Water   15.6% –17.6 %

Proteins and fat-soluble vitamins and minerals 1% –1.2 % include:

- Phosphorus
- Calcium
- Vitamins A, D and E
- Available as salted or unsalted butter   (Ranken, *et al.*, 1997).

Butterfat crystals are classified as existing in the following states

- Alpha (α)
- Beta prime ($\beta!$)
- Beta (β)

The alpha (α) form are the least stable of the butter crystals and have the lowest melting point, and generally scattered randomly in the butter. The beta prime ($\beta!$) or intermediate stage tend to align themselves at right angles in alternating rows and are larger than the alpha crystalline form. They are more stable and have a higher melting point than the alpha crystals. In this form, they form a smooth surface which is ideal for lamination as the smooth crystalline surfaces allow the butter layers to glide and create even layers displaying the best plasticity. The beta (β) crystals are the largest crystalline form in butter and tend to form in parallel rows.

These crystals are the most stable of the three states and have the highest melting point (Brown, 2018). The shape and type of butter crystals govern their practicality in both pastry making and food preparation. A common characteristic of butterfat is that the butter's melting point increases as the crystal size increases. The first form of crystal in butter, the alpha (α) crystal, is the smallest state, the middle-sized crystal is the beta prime (β!) or intermediate stage, to the final and largest stage is the beta (β) crystal (Brown, 2018).

The tempering of butter for croissant sheets takes place at the manufacturing stage of the process. The butter's plasticity and consistency are determined by both the correct tempering and the accurate addition of hard fat balanced by removing oils and liquid components. Tempering rigid butter sheets by passing them through a pastry sheeter or hydraulic press raises the fat's temperature slightly, leading to the alignment and formation of the beta prime crystals in the butterfat, which gives good plasticity during processing and texture to the finished product. The rheological answer of roll-in butter arises from a colloidal grid of different types of fat crystals. The network or matrix formed by the fat's manufacturing process and crystallisation influences its lamination characteristics.

To ensure that good lamination characteristics are maintained throughout the process of making croissants, the crystallisation must be judiciously performed by controlling the temperature of the butter at all times (Rodriguez & Merangioni, 2018). Lamination butter is normally plasticised as it is prepared for incorporation in pastry by a process known in French as beurrage. The butter is placed between a plastic sheet or parchment paper and beaten down with a rolling pin to give plasticity to the butter and also to encourage the formation of small crystals to the butter's crystal network. The most favourable temperature range for working with hard, dry, croissant butter is between 7 °C –11 °C, whereas standard types of butter with lower fat content are most plastic between 16 °C –21 °C (Stamm, 2011). I find the best working temperature with 84% butterfat at about 9 °C.

Desired Dough Temperature

Bakers and pastry chefs make bread and pastry worldwide, from tropical areas to colder locations in the Northern and Southern Hemispheres. This means that daily working temperatures won't be the same for every baker. A baker in Ireland or the UK may come to work to meet flour, sugar, and equipment at 10 °C, whereas a baker in the Bahamas or Namibia may be working with ingredients and equipment at 22 °C. These temperature differences are important because to kick start the gassing process and achieve consistent dough fermentation, it's crucial to ensure the final dough temperature is 24 °C –26 °C, referred to as the DDT. The baker in Ireland may need to warm their ingredients (e.g., flour, water). The baker in Namibia may need to chill their ingredients in a refrigerator overnight before using them.

Luckily, there's a good rule of thumb you can use to roughly calculate the dough temp so that when the dough is finished mixing, it'll be at the desired or optimum temperature to promote fermentation. Generally, when using flour at room temperature, you'll need to adjust the water temperature to achieve the DDT. Every baker should commit this calculation to memory and employ it as part of their daily decision-making processes.

Calculating the Desired Dough Temperature

When calculating DDT, *twice the required dough temperature minus the flour temperature gives you the required water temperature.*

Considered as a formula, the rule looks like this:

$$(DDT \times 2) - \text{Flour Temperature} = \text{Water Temperature}$$

or

$$(DDT \times 2) - FT = WT$$

The formula generally considers the friction factor (i.e., the temperature increase due to the heat generated by a mixer) when mixing the dough. A couple examples may be helpful. Let's use the temperature examples given earlier in this section.

Example 1. Cold climate (10 °C)

The DDT for a particular recipe is 26 °C. Therefore, the bakery temperature, and therefore everything else in the bakery, including your flour, is 10 °C.

$$(DDT \times 2) - FT = WT$$

$$(26\ °C \times 2) - FT = WT$$

$$52\ °C - FT = WT$$

$$52\ °C - 10\ °C = WT$$

$$42\ °C = WT$$

Twice the DDT of 26 °C is 52 °C minus the temperature of the flour (10 °C) gives you the needed temperature of the water (42 °C).

Example 2. Warm climate (22 °C)

The DDT for a particular recipe is 26 °C. Therefore, the bakery temperature, and therefore everything else in the bakery, including your flour, is 22 °C.

$$(DDT \times 2) - FT = WT$$

$$(26\ °C \times 2) - 22\ °C = WT$$

$$52\ °C - 22\ °C = 30\ °C$$

Twice the DDT of 26 °C is 52 °C minus the temperature of the flour (22 °C) gives you the needed temperature of the water (30 °C).

Understanding the Dough

Dough rheology is a science, and it is not my intention to get into its science in this book. Laminated dough generally has a lower hydration level than bread or brioche dough. A good rule of thumb is to use 500 g of total liquid (water/milk/egg combined) per 1,000 g flour or a 50% hydration. If the dough is too soft (overhydrated), it will be challenging to combine the dough and butter as the dough will stretch/flow over the butter like the crest of a wave, giving a large lump of dough at the ends and the sides of the pastry block. If the dough is too tight, cracking and difficulty in processing will occur. If the dough is too warm, the butter will begin to soften/melt into oil, leading to poor lamination when the butter is placed on it. Additionally, if the dough is too cold, it will fracture when passed through a pastry sheeter as the dough will snap.

If the butter is too cold, the butter will also crack, and improper layers which look marbled in appearance will form. The dough and butter should have a similar consistency and temperature, which will aid the formation of desired even layers throughout the pastry. The ideal temperature range for commencing lamination of the dough is between 1.1 °C –3.3 °C. The dough is generally made the previous day and given a short mixing time. The dough should be cold fermented overnight to allow the dough's full development and the relaxation of the mixing process's gluten. The cold fermentation also develops the dough's structure and aromatic qualities, giving the croissant pastry its distinctive taste and texture. The dough should be degassed by hand or through a reversible sheeter and placed in the freezer for a few minutes to ensure that it is at the optimum temperature for further processing. Additionally, this stretching of the dough in the sheeter not only further degasses the dough but it also importantly causes protein alignment of the gluten in one direction. It is important to remember to rotate the pastry 90° at each stage of the lamination, i.e., the lock-in, the first fold, and any subsequent folds. In this way, the pastry is stretched equally in different directions, eliminating shrinkage following final sheeting. Care in the process ensures that the dough/butter layers' laminated structure remains intact throughout the process. In summary, the pastry temperature should be controlled at all stages to arrest all fermentation during the lamination, sheeting and cutting stages until the pastry is placed into the proofer to activate the yeast for the final fermentation phase.

Maintaining A Sourdough Starter

In some of the recipes in this book, I use my sourdough starter, "Covid Culture-2020", to add elasticity, acidity, and depth of flavour to the dough. If you are already a sourdough baker, you will already be familiar with the sourdough process. If not, I will describe the process briefly below. As this book is about laminated pastry, I won't be deviating off the topic much. Still, I will provide step-by-step guidance and detail on making and maintaining your existing starter and when to use it to make the dough for your pastry.

Starter-A Symbiotic Relationship

The wild yeasts, Lactic Acid bacteria's (LABS) and the Acetic Acid bacteria's (AABS), sustain each other's exitance in what is a mutually beneficial or symbiotic relationship in a starter and when used to produce sourdough bread. According to the United States Department of Agriculture's (USDA) database, 100 g of wholemeal flour has approximately 0.4 g of sugar. Enriched white flour has approximately 1.11 g of sugar, of which 0.3 grams is fructose and 0.03 g is glucose. In a mature starter, the wild yeasts feed on these simple sugars and start to break down the flour's starch and convert the starch into glucose and simple sugars. The LABS feed on the simple sugars produced by the wild yeasts, who also produce alcohol as a by-product of fermentation. The AABS feed on the wild yeasts' alcohol to create Acetic Acid, which is desirable in sourdough production.

Qualities of A Good Starter

- ➢ It should be reliable and consistent when fed and when the dough is made.
- ➢ It should have good tolerance and impart both good flavour and strength into the bread made from it.
- ➢ The bread and starter's aroma should be pleasant and balanced, neither too bland nor too sour.
- ➢ Acetic Acid's: Lactic Acid ratios should be roughly 1 part of Acetic Acidic to 3 parts of Lactic Acid. These ratios are generally accepted as being the best balance of the established starter colony.

Starter pH

Typically, the pH of a mature starter culture ranges between 3.9 to a pH of 4.1. If using whole grain rye flour or wholemeal to feed a starter, it will be more acidic than when only white wheat flour is used to feed the starter due to the many additional nutrients and wild yeasts present in the rye flour.

Recipe for Starter Refresh Example

Ingredients	Quantity	Ratio
Strong flour	20 g	2
Water (40 °C –42 °C)	20 g	2
Liquid starter culture	10 g	1
Total	50 g	

What If I Only Use My Sourdough Once A Week?

If you are only using your sourdough once per week to bake, you should feed the sourdough as above, but then place it into a refrigerator, covered at 3 °C –4 °C. This will slow down the starter, and it will go into suspended animation/storage mode. When you plan on baking again, take the starter out of the refrigerator the day before, refeed it, leave it overnight, and make the dough the following day with the refreshed starter. It's a good idea to know what weight of starter you have. By keeping several clean glass jars, you can weigh your starter into a clean jar and label it.

Notes on Refreshing

The flour you use in your starter will determine the flavour of your starter and your bread and pastry.

You can choose to refresh using

- ➢ Rye and baker's flour for brown/seeded loaves

- Bakers flour and wholemeal flour for wholegrain and seeded loaves
- Just baker's flour for classic white sourdough

It is important to keep the ratios of the flour the same all the time.

The temperature of your room and the water you use will speed up the rate of fermentation when the room or the water used to refresh is hotter, and it will slow down fermentation when the water used or the area the starter is stored in is colder. You will always have to adjust these factors, both seasonally and depending on your bakery or room's ambient temperature.

Sourdough Main Points

Sourdough is a living thing. It requires care, as every living thing does, to get the best out of it. Think of it as a farm animal/domestic animal; it requires water, food, warmth, shelter (a container to live in) and consistency to thrive!

Equipment List

- Container - a small jar with a lid or a clear plastic container with a lid.
- Spatula or spoons /or /and digital scales if you have one. If not, we use teaspoons!
- Wholemeal flour unbleached; untreated, or wholemeal rye flour and bakers flour unbleached untreated.
- Probe digital thermometer.
- Warm, filtered water.
- Elastic band to monitor growth.
- A sticky label to name your sourdough (mine is called Covid Culture 2020) and record the weight.
- A warm place to leave it to ferment.

1. Good Hygiene: Wash your hands, and any other implements, such as spoons, wooden spoons, stirrers/spatulas, before you start. Weigh/measure all ingredients accurately, mix well together using the end of a spoon or spatula.

2. Use a clean Kilner jar with a lid (no gasket needed), glass bolognese or jam jar or a plastic container with a lid, washed in hot soapy water, rinsed thoroughly and dried.

3. Do not seal the lid. This allows the CO_2 gas produced by the sourdough's fermentation to release into the atmosphere.

4. Do not use a metal container as the Acid generated by the sourdough will react with the metal creating corrosion of the metal and giving the sourdough a horrible metallic taste and discolour it.

5. Flour: Use organic, untreated wholegrain flours, wheat, spelt rye, or other ancient grains such as Einkorn, Durum. In fact, all grains can be used to make a sourdough starter.

6. Probe or a digital thermometer to ensure a consistent feeding water temperature.

7. Warm filtered water:

- Tap water contains chlorine/fluoride, which is put there to kill bacteria. We want to preserve and encourage the wild yeasts and bacteria to grow. Using filtered water, we help the process by filtering out any harmful added chemicals to the tap water, which may delay the wild yeasts and bacteria's action in your sourdough.
- If tap water is left to stand for a few days, depending on the levels of treatment by your local water supply, the evaporation time of added chlorine from tap water can be projected; it is estimated that the roughly 2 ppm of chlorine in tap water will take up to 5 days or around 120 hours to evaporate from 10 US gallons of water when left to stand in an open container.
- If you don't have a water filter, you can boil the tap water for 15 minutes and cool it before use. This process is expensive and should only be used as a last resort.
- You can use bottled, filtered water, just ensure there is no chlorine present in your starter.

Wild yeasts and the Lactobacilli are sensitive to temperature. By being consistent with the water temperature, the sourdough will learn to ferment consistently. By initially adding warm water (50 °C) to the flours each time, the warmth will stimulate the bacteria and wild yeasts in the developing sourdough to promote fermentation. The sourdough temperature will be approximately 30 °C–32 °C, which is ideal for the growing sourdough. Your sourdough will become its own unique colony of microflora, wild yeasts, and bacteria with many uses in bread and pastry baking, so care for it.

Days 1-3, the feeding quantities and the water feeding temperatures of 45 °C–50 °C are maintained and remain the same. By day three, carbon dioxide gas will be visible, and the sourdough will begin developing acetic tones when you smell it.

Day 4, the quantities of water and flour are doubled as the natural fermentation begins to be visible. The microorganisms are growing and require extra food and water. The water temperature is reduced in temperature to between 20 °C–25 °C, slowing down and controlling the fermentation.

Day 5 The quantities of flours and water are again maintained as double the day one quantity. The water is added at 20 °C–25 °C. When mixed, the dough is left to ferment overnight for 24 hours. The sourdough is now maturing and has many visible bubbles of CO2 gas, and has an acidy note when smelled.

Process of Preparation

1. Using a clean bowl, whisk the starter and the warm water together, add the flour and mix well to wet all the flour. Place in a clean glass jar with a lid loosely fitted.
2. Allow the starter to ferment at a warm room temperature of 26 °C –28 °C for about 6 hours before use. Pour it into the dough-making water. It should float. Whisk them together with the yeast in the recipe, then make your dough.
3. Allow the remaining starter to complete fermentation and transfer the liquid sourdough to the refrigerator at 4 °C after 18 hours of fermentation.

Important Liquid Sourdough Makeup Points

Adding warm water to the starter will stimulate the starter to activate with the water's liquid and warmth. Adding the flour provides the food source for the starter to feed and grow. I always use a glass jar for hygiene reasons when growing starters, and I mark the starter's level with an elastic band. It provides a good visual indicator to watch the performance of the liquid sourdough as it grows. An active sourdough should at least double if not triple in size. If you think of your starter as a pet or farm animal and tend to it in this manner of thought, it needs water, food, attention and warmth to thrive. Additionally, like any relationship, it requires consistency to keep it fresh and healthy and prevent it from falling sour.

Holding Back Some Sourdough Starter

You should always hold back some of your starter for making more sourdough for future baking. Keep half the weight of what you require. When your starter begins to be large enough, say after day three, after feeding the starter. Place an elastic band over the jar or container you are using and mark the starter level you have just mixed. You can monitor its progress overnight and see whether it has doubled or tripled in volume since you fed it last.

Storage of Liquid Sourdough

Sourdough should be kept in a sealed jar in the refrigerator at 3 °C –4 °C. It can be stored for several days, but no more than a week in this state, and then refreshed again later as described earlier. The stored liquid sourdough can also be used as an ingredient in the pastry dough.

The Need to Rotate Pastry Through 90 ° On Each New Sheeting Fold

When making all types of laminated pastry, it is essential to rotate the pastry block at a 90° angle on each rolling stage throughout the process after folding. The science behind this is that the gluten matrix aligns in a two-dimensional phase and form long elastic chains when stretched in one direction. If you can imagine, as a child, having an elastic band in your hand and you stretch it, then release the tension, the elastic band returns to the shape it has been formed into. However, if you keep stretching it harder and harder, the elastic band will eventually snap and shatter. The elastic band's return to its original shape is known as elastic recoil, and this can be seen when making pastry as a shrinking of the sheeted pastry when folding or cutting. The elastic limit of a rubber band is the limit at which it will snap and lose its original form if stretched beyond this point.

Dough reacts similarly during lamination. By rotating the pastry through 90° each time you are sheeting the pastry, you stretch and realign the dough's gluten matrix at a right angle to the previous sheeting stage of the pastry making. Resting is also more important as it allows the pastry block time to recover its elasticity from the rolling and sheeting phase. Following the lock-in, the pastry is sheeted and folded. The black arrows below in the diagram indicate the direction that the gluten matrix in the pastry is being stretched. To balance the elasticity and create an elastic equilibrium throughout the pastry, preventing shrinkage is vital. The pastry needs to be stretched equally in all directions, hence the need to rotate the pastry 90° during each sheeting cycle.

The arrows in the diagram indicate the stretching and the resistance of the gluten matrix, or elastic recoil 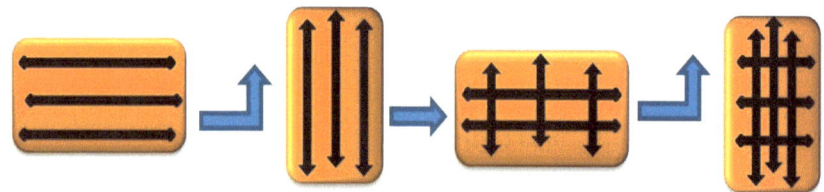 acting in the pastry as it is processed. As the gluten matrix stretches, so does it develop resistance and pull back, much like stretching an elastic band and releasing it. In this way, an elastic equilibrium is established within the pastry, and the pastry is in balance. Shrinking is neutralised by even forces acting within the pastry by this gluten matrix when rotated and sheeted in opposite directions during the make up process.

Proofing Pastry in The Home

While the recipe, make up, and shaping of yeasted laminated pastry are deemed by most as the hardest part of making this style of pastry, all the hard work invested in making it can be lost by incorrect proofing. The proofing process can be a deal-breaker as to whether you end up with a perfect honeycomb structure or not. Many home bakers do not have the luxury of temperature and humidity-controlled proofers to use as a tool in producing exceptional pastry.

There is the small Brød & Taylor home proofer/yoghurt maker; I have posted a link on it in the other online resources section at the end of the book. It is expensive but has great ratings from those who have purchased it, and it can be used to make yoghurt, hold melted chocolate, and folds away to the size of a large book for storage when finished using it. If you cannot buy one, or it is not in the budget, don't worry. Proofing can be achieved in a variety of ways. If you live in a warm/humid climate, for example, or work in a warm home or kitchen, simply covering the pastries in a plastic bag to prevent skinning will work just fine. You can prevent the proofing pastry from sticking to the plastic by standing inverted tall glasses spaced out on your baking trays. The pastry can also be placed (again covered) in a hot press or airing cupboard.

Proofing can also be achieved using a domestic oven with a few careful procedures, and I will outline a sample procedure below. The thing to understand about proofing is that there are two very important elements at play in the proofing process:

1. Heat (to stimulate fermentation or gassing in the dough)
2. Humidity (to prevent skinning of the dough and allow maximum expansion in proof)

The heat stimulates the yeast but cannot be too warm; otherwise, the yeast will perish. The butter layers will also melt if the temperature is too high. Humidity prevents the expanding pastry from skinning on the surface, and therefore expansion of the pastries can occur. If there is no humidity, a thick skin will form on the outer surfaces, and the pastry will not be able to proof/expand properly due to the hard skin surrounding it. Most domestic ovens have a light. Check and see what temperature your oven generates with just the light left on after 1 hour. Use an accurate probe thermometer where possible. If it gets too hot after 1 hour (over 28 °C), reduce the time.

Additionally, many ovens have a defrost cycle which can be pre-programmed to very low temperatures of 20 °C –30 °C. If these pre-sets exist on your domestic oven, humidity can be introduced by pouring boiling water into a small tray placed at the bottom of the oven. Be sure to place your tray of pastries in the middle deck of the oven, pour the boiling water into the bottom tray and close the oven door.

Another simple way of proofing where you have adequate heat and no humidity is to prove the pastries in a deep tin. Simply place the pastries into the deep pan shape, egg wash and wrap the baking tin tightly in clingfilm. Finally, no matter which technique you use to proof the pastry, it may take some hours, and patience is essential. Do not bake the pastry until you can see the layers separating and the pastry jiggles like wobbly jelly when shaken gently; jiggle videos are in the resources section at the end of the book.

Baking Using Different Oven Types

The heat source and balance of that heat in the oven are critical to getting a good bake. As the pastry heats up in the oven, the water in the dough and the butter layers vaporises from water into steam. As the steam trapped in the layers expands, the dough inflates, and the layers created separate from each other, giving volume to the pastry. Lipids in the butter basically fry the pastry, resulting in light, airy, flaky puff paste and viennoiserie qualities. Bakers bake in different ovens all over the world. Some are domestic ovens for home baking, some are commercial ovens built robustly for heavy-duty work. In my baking experiences in various countries, bakeries, and schools, all the ovens I have used have their own unique quirkiness for over three decades.

Generally, to clarify my statement, ovens are made mainly of metal, insulation, glass, stone, and various electric or gas components to generate heat for baking. They have doors made of thermal glass, metal, or both, which allow the baker to load/unload and see into the baking chamber while baking. All ovens are screwed or welded together, metal on metal; over time, due to this expansion/contraction, the oven's insulation and thermal efficiency can deteriorate. I am not covering brick or wood-fired ovens as they are generally not used for baking viennoiserie. All ovens are, by their nature, subjected to the extremes of heating and cooling daily. As ovens age, all this heating and cooling can cause the oven to be less efficient than a new oven as the metal in the ovens/door seals, the screws and welds holding it together, and heating elements suffer wear and tear with continued use.

Insulation can also deteriorate, causing further heat differentials. Thermostats can again fail or give the baker erroneous readings of the actual oven temperature. A small stand-alone oven thermometer can be purchased in most kitchenware shops and verify an ovens existing thermometers integrity. Ovens can develop hot and cold spots, and a baker using an oven daily gets to know their oven very well. The oven operator can see that perhaps the oven's back left is cooler than the front left and knows to rotate the trays in this part of the oven halfway through the bake to get an even colour on a batch of baked goods. An infrared (IR) thermometer is an excellent and useful tool for measuring oven temperature. The book's baking temperatures reflect the oven temperatures I have baked with and my experience in using commercial ovens daily.

Most small viennoiserie pieces bake in deck ovens at 200 °C for roughly 20 minutes and in convection ovens at 175 °C for 16–18 minutes. Commercial electric multi-deck ovens also have separate controls for the heating elements of the top, bottom, and door of each deck in the oven. The controls range from a figure of 1 to 10 in baking intensity, with 1 being the lowest or gentlest heat setting and 10 being the most intense heat. The settings for baking viennoiserie on these deck ovens are Top heat 7, bottom heat 1 to 2, and door heat 6 to 7. But, please bear in mind that all ovens are different and heat/bake differently. Use a second stand-alone thermometer to check that the oven thermometer to cross-check and calibrate your oven.

Every oven will lose temperature when you open the door, especially convection ovens. That said, they also recover quicker than deck ovens and are the professionals' choice of oven for baking viennoiserie. Viennoiserie generally has almost 1/3rd more volume when baked in a convection oven than the same product baked in a deck oven. This is due to the rapid recovery to temperature of convection ovens. The fan accelerated air within, which can quickly penetrate the pastry, heats the core rapidly, and reduces bake time. Deck ovens are mainly used in baking bread and confectionery. They are not as good at baking viennoiserie as a fan oven, as the heat method is known as a dead heat bake, i.e. heat conducted by the oven sole and roof via electrical elements on the top and the chamber itself.

There is commonly no fan in a deck oven, but some superior and expensive commercial models have fans for each deck, too. Deck ovens are better at retaining heat than convection ovens, but they can take a very long time to recover the heat lost during loading the oven if it is set too low. I have witnessed an oven at 220 °C, fully loaded with bread drop to 150 °C and take 30 minutes to return to 220 °C. Temperature and time considerations need to be made, whether you fully load an oven or are only baking one tray in the oven as the partially filled oven will bake one tray faster than, say, three and lose less heat in loading. As the oven door is open a shorter time, and the weight of one tray and product will heat faster than three times that. For example, when you put a tray of pastry into an oven, the weight of the metal tray plus the weight of the pastries you are baking will rob the oven of some of its heat. The oven will lose 20 °C to 50 °C, depending on the oven type and whether the oven is filled to capacity or only has one tray in it after loading. All these factors will determine the oven recovery time, which will be unique to your particular oven. The pastries will be baked at a much lower heat as the oven struggles to rise in temperature; the thermostat will be calling for heat all the time. The net result is a longer bake time, inferior product, and a drier product, as baking at a lower temperature longer will dry out the product. A working example of the above is when I fill my convection oven with croissants.

1. There are 6 trays at 800 g each = 4,800 g of metal

2. A total of 60 pastries at 70 g = 4,200 g of pastry

That's 9,000 g of room temperature materials that require heating up to my bake temperature of 170 °C. It's like chucking ice into a drink. It cools it down rapidly. It takes a lot of time to transfer enough energy into the tins and product to get back up to the correct baking temperature. For example, I set the convection oven at 220 °C, load it, close the oven door and reset the thermostat to 170 °C to bake my product. If I did not do this, the oven temperature would fall to 120 °C and the products would not be very nice due to longer bake time, drying out, and would lose that boldness in the bake that a sharp, hot oven gives to products. The oven I use drops over 50 °C after loading, so I always factor for this when baking. Becoming familiar with your own oven is easy by simply measuring the oven temperature drop when loaded fully. An Infrared IR thermometer is an excellent tool for establishing this.

The Bakers' Percentage Explained

Many people simply have a blockage when it comes to numbers. I have many people request online to explain the bakers' percentage or bakers' maths as it is also known. If you can count to 10, you can do it! If you can count to 100, it will be the easiest thing you ever did. Bakers maths or Bakers% simply mean that the main ingredient, flour in all their forms in a recipe, such as wholemeal, white, rye etc., is always 100%. All other ingredients are measured against the quantity of flour in the recipe. While weight quantities can go up or down according to mix or batch sizes, the percentages will always remain constant. If you have a great recipe, it can be scaled up to commercial quantities or down for home baking without the recipe altering in any way as the percentages maintain the exact ratios of ingredients during the conversion. The hydration of dough is the percentage of total liquids in a recipe in relation to total flour weight. The usual liquids used in pastry making include water, egg, and milk. I have included both water and egg in this exercise to demonstrate hydration levels in a dough. Below, I set out an example of recipe conversion with bakers' percentage, which can be applied to all recipes:

Sample Bread Recipe Expressed in Bakers %

Ingredient	Weight in g small recipe	Bakers %	Weight in g large recipe
Bread flour	80	80%	8,000
Wholemeal	20	20%	2,000
Flour total:	100	100%	10,000
Water	68	68%	6,800
Egg	5	5%	500
Hydration total:	73	73%	7,300
Salt	2	2%	200
Butter	4	4%	400
Fresh yeast	2	2%	200

To break down the recipe's main components, I have separately analysed two types of flour and two types of liquid to measure the dough's hydration accurately. The above example uses 100g of flour in the recipe, 80% white flour and 20% wholemeal and is expressed as a combined total being 100%. Water 68% and egg 5% combine to give a collective hydration figure of 73%. All other ingredients are similarly expressed, salt 2%, butter 4%, and fresh yeast 2%. By examining the bakers' % at first glance, the baker can ascertain whether the dough is highly hydrated (over 70%) or, in the case of croissant dough, a stiff dough of 50% hydration. Depending on flour types used in a pastry recipe, I have successfully made croissant with varying hydration levels and recommend a hydration level of between 46%–57% depending on flour strength and flours' adsorption ability (damaged starch in the milling process increases its adsorption abilities). Below is a viennoiserie recipe for croissant pastry I have used many times. I created an expanded recipe spreadsheet that includes all ingredients in the recipe, the weight in grams, and the Bakers % ingredient.

Additionally, I include the batch yield, the total % butter in the pastry, which includes the butter in the dough, plus lamination butter. Finally, I have colour coded the spreadsheet below–flour is gold, liquids are blue, and butter is, of course, yellow. The hydration is 50% in this sample recipe.

Base Croissant Recipe

Ingredients	1 Mix	1/2 Mix	Bakers %	Hydration %
	Kg / g	Kg / g	500	50.00
Overnight dough Stage 1				
Strong flour	500	250	100.0 %	
Egg	50	25	10.0 %	
Water	200	100	40.0 %	
Sugar	45	23	9.0 %	
Fresh yeast	35	18	7.0 %	
Milk powder	25	13	5.0 %	
Salt	7	4	1.4 %	
Butter	25	13	5.0 %	
Dough head weight	887	444	Butter on Dough %	Total Butter % in both Dough & Lamination
Lamination dough Stage 2				
Laminating butter	225	113	25.4	30.4
Total batch weight	1,112	556		
Yield	15	7		
Scaling wt in grams	75			

Core Temperature and Chilling Pastry Using Ice Blankets

A crucial part of good pastry making is to control both the dough's fermentation and the butter's temperature throughout the makeup process. It is essential to prevent pastry skinning or proofing throughout the lamination stage as uneven layers will form in the pastry from this skin. By using various means of cooling the pastry, fermentation is delayed; both the dough and the butter remain cool throughout the process. Industrial refrigerators, freezers, blast chillers and Cryopack® ice blankets are essential tools for pastry production. In many professional kitchens and bakeries, they have an airconditioned room to control the environmental temperature for pastry consistency. Most home bakers do not have the luxury of such space or equipment. Even in many culinary schools lacking equipment such as blast chillers, it is common practice to simply wrap the pastry in a plastic sheet and chill it down on a metal tray in the freezer. It is essential to wrap the pastry in a thick plastic sheet to prevent frostbite on the surface. Additionally, when using the ice blankets, the plastic keeps the pastry from becoming wet and sticky. When the pastry is chilled in this way, the bottom part of the pastry in contact with the frozen tray will begin to cool rapidly through touching or conduction. The sides and top of the pastry take longer to chill as they rely on the circulation of chilled air or convection to cool them, which creates an imbalance in the chilling process. Often, the bottom, corners and edges of the pastry begin to freeze quicker than the rest of the pastry and cause problems when processing. The freezing is not even throughout the pastry block, and in different areas, the pastry has different temperatures.

It is critical that the pastry is chilled quickly and not frozen during the makeup process, as freezing damages water crystals both in the dough and the water and fat crystals in the butter. If frozen, the dough portion of the pastry will split and crack, and the butter element will become hard, brittle and shatter into pieces, giving a marbled aspect to the pastry and destroying the layers created in the makeup process. Pastry makers in the past have often used two frozen metal trays to chill pastry down quickly. The trays, placed like a sandwich on the sheeted pastry top and bottom, cool the pastry's outside layers quickly. However, the pastry rapidly takes all the coldness out of the trays, and they need to be chilled several times again to be effective at maintaining a low temperature.

A modern approach is to use "Cryopack® Ice Blankets". These are available on Amazon and are worth the investment to serious pastry makers. For home bakers or hobbyists, two packs of frozen corn or peas work equally well as ice blankets, for small quantities of pastry which is an inexpensive option and yields excellent results https://youtu.be/-WZ9w0gPjyg. I first saw the use of ice blankets in pastry processing at the Coupe du Monde de la Boulangerie competitions, Paris, in the mid-2000s by team USA's viennoiserie candidate Peter Yuen and some of the Asian viennoiserie candidates. Ice blankets are excellent for rapidly chilling down laminated pastry as the pastry block is encapsulated top and bottom, physically touching the ice blanket. As a result of this direct contact between pastry and the ice blanket, a very efficient, uniform and rapid chilling of the pastry dough block is possible.

In the illustration page 45, a folded block of pastry (gold) is illustrated with a book fold or a 4, and it is wrapped in an ice blanket (blue). The pastry is touching the ice blanket surface, and it is this direct contact that chills the pastry down quickly. The thicker the pastry, the longer it takes to chill to the core. On the left side of the diagram, the pastry block is much thicker (30 mm) than the one on the right (15 mm). The thick black line illustrates the core or centre of the pastry block. The pastry chills from the outside into the core; when wrapped in ice blankets, pastry has the dual effect of cooling by the ice blankets top and bottom.

When inserted into the ice blanket, the pastry's thickness is important, as the thinner it is, the more rapidly the pastry will chill down. In the diagram on the left, the ice blanket needs to chill through 15 mm of pastry top and bottom, and there is a danger that the pastry will begin to move/proof in the core before it can be influenced by the chilling of the ice blanket. On the right side of the illustration, the same pastry block is sheeted down to 15 mm. The ice blanket must only chill through 7.5 mm of pastry to get to the core, and as a result, it cools twice as quickly. Therefore, I always recommend sheeting folded pastry to between 12 mm–15 mm before chilling in ice blankets.

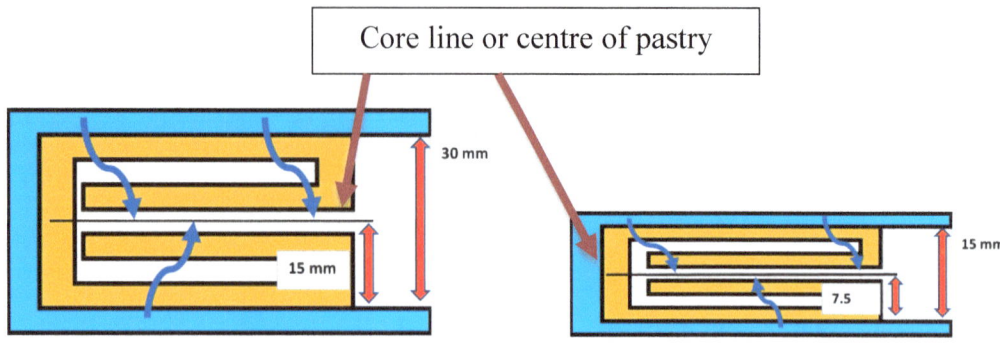

Understanding Core Temperature in Proofing Pastry

As discussed in understanding the core temperature in chilling pastry earlier, the centre of something is generally referred to as the core or the middle. Any pastry that is rolled up when shaping, such as croissant, pain chocolate, and pain aux raisin, will have a spiral profile with layers coiled on top of each other, a core, and an outside. Pastry is a poor conductor of heat, and so its outside will rise to the temperature of the proofer faster than its core. This problem is exacerbated by pastry shapes whose cores are far from their outsides, such as the croissant and pain au chocolat. The outside of the pastry in a proofer will slowly begin to heat up, but it will take some time for the heat to permeate throughout the pastry to the core. Generally, croissant pastry is proofed at approximately 26 °C –27 °C for 2 –3 hours. It is impossible to prove croissant pastry at a higher temperature, as the butter will melt inside the layers and fold to oil, destroying the layers created during lamination. As illustrated in the core pastry diagram on the next page, the outside surface begins to heat up and proof.

It takes time for the proofer heat to get to the pastry's core and heat it up. Honeycomb crumb structure is a good indicator of a successfully proofed pastry. A thick and gummy, non-aerated core indicates insufficient proof time and baking the pastry before the pastry core has opened out and proofed fully. It is possibly the most common fault in baking laminated yeasted pastry.

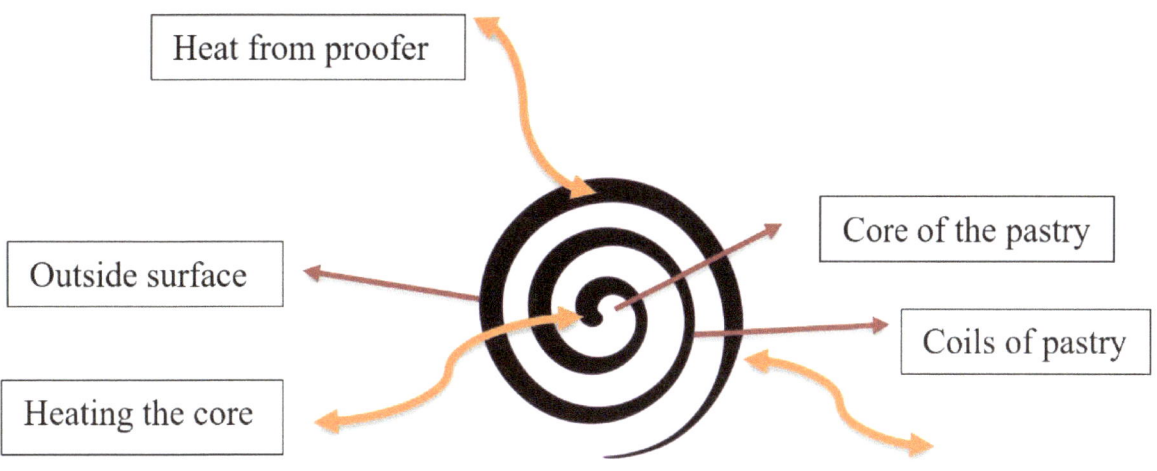

Recipes Used in This Publication

I have relied on many different recipes in this book. All of them work very well and have slight variances between them. I do not have one favourite recipe as they all serve to further my existing studies and understanding of pastry making. Additionally, professional bakers and home bakers alike will have their own favourite recipes and secret ingredients. Still, they can apply many of the book's techniques to improve the outcomes of their own products and procedures. Knowledge, practice and consistency are key elements in perfecting laminated pastry making. Hydration of 48% –52% of the dough will give a dough easy to handle and hold its form and shape easily. My own personal target hydration is approximately 50 % for mostly all of the laminated pastry that I make with Irish flour, but this may require adjustment depending on the country, the flour available, and the flour's strength. If you increase hydration beyond this, the dough is sticky and requires a lot of dusting flour. It does not keep its shape well and will flow in proof spreading out on the tray as it bakes and generally not as bold as lower hydrated pastry. The visibility of layers is also affected by increased hydration; something to consider!

Processing Factors

- A poolish preferment may be used in the main dough up to a maximum of 10% dough weight if your flour is very strong as it adds elasticity and flavour to the dough.
- Pâté fermentée can also be added to the dough and also adds flavour and elasticity.
- Dough mixing times mentioned are using a standard Hobart type mixer with a dough hook: 4 minutes on 1st speed, 4 –5 minutes on 2nd speed. Times will vary depending on the machine type.
- After mixing, the dough is covered with plastic and given five minutes of bulk fermentation at room temperature. Sheet out the dough to between 12 mm –15 mm. Wrap the dough in plastic and place in the refrigerator overnight at a temperature of between 3 °C –4 °C for 12 –16 hours.
- A cold fermentation process gives the best flavour, and both relaxes and strengthens the dough, imparting good elasticity for processing and lamination
- Dough hydration should be a figure of between 48% –51%, depending on the type of flour used.
- Ideally, the dough and butter should have roughly the same consistency when sheeting.
- In the morning, upon taking the fermented dough from the refrigerator, DO NOT KNEAD/MANIPULATE THE DOUGH! Otherwise, you will toughen the dough, and it will shrink from elastic recoil.
- Simply flatten it down with a rolling pin and sheet out the dough to 10 mm, wrap it in plastic and place it in the freezer for 10 minutes.
- The dough should be chilled to as close to 3 °C before locking in the butter.
- Butter should ideally be shaped into one thin rectangular block the day before and stored in a refrigerator. Before use, take the butter out of the refrigerator and leave it aside for a few minutes to soften slightly. It should be malleable, like putty and not hard or brittle. Bend it before placing it on the dough. If it is stiff, wait a few minutes.

- ➢ **A YouTube video tutorial on how to make the butter block on a pastry sheeter is attached in the link below**

- ➢ The butter is ready for lamination when of plastic consistency roughly at a temperature of 7 °C –11 °C. Prod the butter with a finger, and if the finger makes an indentation without melting the butter, it is ready for use (see it in the video).

- ➢ The butter and dough in the pastry increase in temperature due to outside atmospheric temperature and the friction of rolling the dough. On mechanical sheeters, the pastry's temperature can increase by as much as 1 °C per pass from the friction alone.

How To Prepare A Butter Block On YouTube

Follow the link: https://youtu.be/Cj0gEXtXexw

Lock-In and Lamination Numbering System

There is much confusion over the names, the types of folds used, and the number of folds used in pastry making. The universal numbering system is a more accurate and appropriate method of describing and defining how the pastry is folded after the butter is added to the dough. Numbers are international and provide a global understanding of lamination sequences. The first stage is always known as the lock-in phase. The lock-in number will always appear as a bold number at the beginning of a sequence, for example, like a **3** or a **5** in this book to instil the universal numbering system's learning objective. There are two composite ingredient components in laminated pastry making systems:

1. A dough component
2. A fat/butter component

The two components mentioned above are the same for puff pastry production. The only difference is that in the case of croissant dough, the dough is yeasted. For lamination to take place, the butter/fat must be encapsulated into the lock-in is referred to as the first number in the sequence of pastry making, which, as mentioned above, will be highlighted and identified in bold text throughout this document. The first number in the pastry laminating system is always the lock-in number where you "lock-in" the butter block between the dough, literally sandwiching the butter block between layers of dough

Dough Touching Points

If you take a piece of dough in your fingers, stretch it, fold it over on itself and compress/squeeze it, it does not form two separate layers of dough. Many of us have experienced this phenomenon as children while chewing, stretching gum in our mouths and fingers. The force of compression on the dough and the dough's stickiness causes the two outside dough layers to bond and become one dough layer. Applying this principle to croissant pastry making as the dough encapsulates the butter and is rolled out to create a thin sheet of pastry, the dough always remains outside the pastry. The butter is always remaining in between the formed dough layers. When the sheeted dough is folded into a book form 4 or a half fold 3, the outside dough layers stack on top of each other, and these two layers or pleats of dough I refer to as a "Dough Touching Point" or DTP for short.

When compressed by rolling, the two dough touching points become one layer of dough. As a result, you must factor in this disappearance of one layer when calculating total layers in the pastry during each folding process. The formula is very simple and straightforward. You subtract one layer from the total number of layers for each dough touching point. Given that the most common folding forms are a 4-fold or a 3-fold, the maths become easy. Applying this principle to any number of folds, the following numbers apply for exact layer calculation.

- A 6-fold has five Dough Touching Points minus 5 layers
- A 5-fold has four Dough Touching Points minus 4 layers
- A 4-fold has three Dough Touching Points minus 3 layers
- A 3-fold has two Dough Touching Points minus 2 layers
- A 2-fold has one Dough Touching Point minus 1 layer

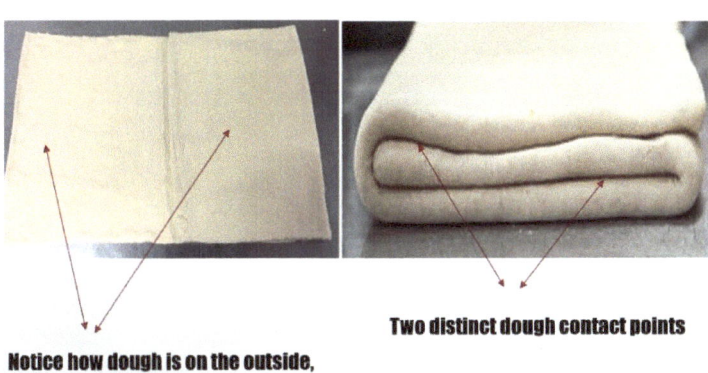

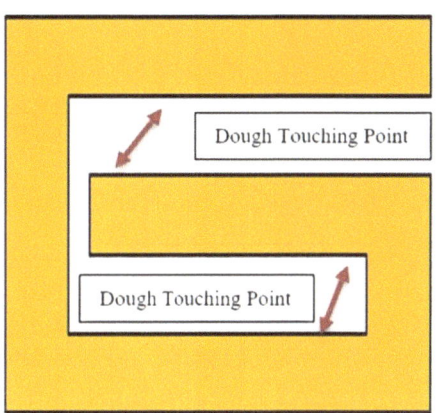

Steps And Stages of Preparing Fermented Laminated Pastry

3-4-3 System Process Overview

The **3-4-3** system is possibly the most popular and widespread used sequence of lamination in the world. It is used for the croissant, pain aux raisins, chocolatines, and many other pastry types. When completed, the pastry will have 25 alternating layers of dough and butter. It produces a lovely leafy exterior and a honeycombed interior. While there are many stages and ingredient choices used in making laminated pastry, overleaf is a bulleted introduction and overview of the procedures/sequence/sequences used to turn raw materials of dough and butter into a finished pastry block. I will cover different recipes and several different lamination systems in later chapters of the book, such as:

1. **3-4-3 (3-3-4) (5-6)** 25 layers (all have the same quantity of layers)
2. **5-4-3** 49 layers
3. **-3-4-4** 33 layers (used for Chocolatine)
4. **-3-3-3 / 3** 55 layers (the / indicates a mandatory rest period)

Additionally, I will cover twin lamination, cross lamination, multi-colour cross lamination and bicolor pastries. These specific lamination systems will be explained in greater detail. Classic croissant making typically employs the **3**-4-3 system. Still, generally, once the first stage - the lock in is complete, the pastry is sheeted (rolled out into a thin sheet) and folded into pleats of pastry into a rectangular block; the purpose of which is to build up a structure of alternating dough/butter/dough layers. These alternating layers give the pastry its structure and impart flakiness and lightness when combined with controlled fermentation. It is most important to always completely wrap the pastry in plastic to prevent the outer dough surface's skinning throughout the process. I have included a YouTube video on how to do this properly. The basic steps employed for a **3**-4-3 system are as follows:

- Mixing of the dough and preparation of the butter block while the dough mixes
- Overnight fermentation of the dough in a refrigerator 3 °C –4 °C
- Pinning out the dough to a rectangle and placing the butter block on the dough
- Sealing the butter block between two layers of dough (**3** lock-in) like a sandwich
- Locking in the butter between the dough to create alternate dough/butter layers
- Sheeting out the lock-in to a thickness of approximately 3.5 mm –4 mm
- The 1st fold of the pastry using a 4-fold (book fold)
- Resting of the pastry in the freezer
- Sheeting out the pastry with its 1st fold to a thickness of approximately 6 mm
- The 2nd fold or folding of the pastry using a 3-fold (half turn)
- Pinning the pastry out to 12 mm and covering in plastic
- Resting of the pastry block in the freezer
- Sheeting out the pastry in preparation for cutting; cutting and shaping of the pastry
- Proofing of the pastry; egg washing the pastry, baking and cooling.

Production of Laminated Croissant Pastry – Sample Recipe

- Disperse yeast, sugar and egg in water, whisk together with a hand whisk
- Add liquid to the flour and other ingredients and mix to a dough

Dough Stage: Sieve the flour, milk powder and salt together, rub the butter into the flour. The dough should be mixed on a 20-quart Hobart-type mixing machine using a dough hook attachment. Mixing times of 2 minutes on 1st speed and 6 minutes on 2nd speed is recommended (Yankellow, 2005). But as always, different flour characteristics will determine mixing times. The dough's shorter mixing time allows for the shearing action that the dough will encounter when final processing through the pastry sheeter or with a rolling pin is given to the dough. The mixed dough should be kneaded into a ball, placed into a container that will allow for the dough's expansion during the cold fermentation process and sealed tight or covered with plastic to prevent skinning (Yankellow, 2005). The dough should be fermented for 45 minutes at room temperature, rolled into a rectangle, covered in plastic, followed by overnight fermentation in a refrigerator at a temperature of 3 °C –6 °C (Vernet, 2020). The focus of this book is butter croissant pastry. Still, vegan croissants can easily be made by substituting the milk/egg/butter in the recipes with water/dairy-free/egg-free ingredients and pastry margarine or vegan butter for the lamination.

Base Croissant Recipe

Ingredients	1 Mix	1/2 Mix	Bakers %	Hydration %
	Kg / g	Kg / g	500	50.00
Overnight dough Stage 1				
Strong flour	500	250	100.0 %	
Egg	50	25	10.0 %	
Water	200	100	40.0 %	
Sugar	45	23	9.0 %	
Fresh yeast	35	18	7.0 %	
Milk powder	25	13	5.0 %	
Salt	7	4	1.4 %	
Butter	25	13	5.0 %	
Dough head weight	887	444	Butter on Dough %	Total Butter % in both Dough & Lamination
Lamination dough Stage 2				
Laminating butter	225	113	25.4	30.4
Total batch weight	1,112	556		
Yield	15	7		
Scaling wt in grams	75			

Lesson #1 the 3-4-3 system

Pros And Cons Of Pastry Made On This System:

25 layers, very flaky externally, very open leafy honeycomb internal texture. It is the easiest of the three systems explained in this book to laminate by hand due to the smaller quantity of layers and least resistance developed in the folding process. This system is less elastic than a **3**-4-4; **5**-4-3 or **3**-3-3-3 system.

Process Method 3-4-3

The fermented dough is then degassed by sheeting it through a pastry sheeter set to 10 mm –12 mm thick, wrapped in plastic to prevent skinning, and placed in a freezer to stiffen the dough chill it close to 0 °C for 30 minutes (Vernet, 2020). The dough is then taken from the freezer and formed into an even rectangle twice the butter block's size. The butter block is placed in the dough rectangle centre as illustrated below, and the centre is sealed by pinching the dough together, leaving the ends exposed with butter showing at each end.

The Lock-In 3

The pastry contains three layers, two dough layers on the top and bottom, with the centre's butter layer. The dough to the pastry block sides can also be sliced to ease elastic recoil and is referred to as the sandwich method. The first stage of this process is known as the "Lock-in"; the butter is locked in between two dough layers.

The dough can be rolled to twice the butter's width and simply folded over in half like a

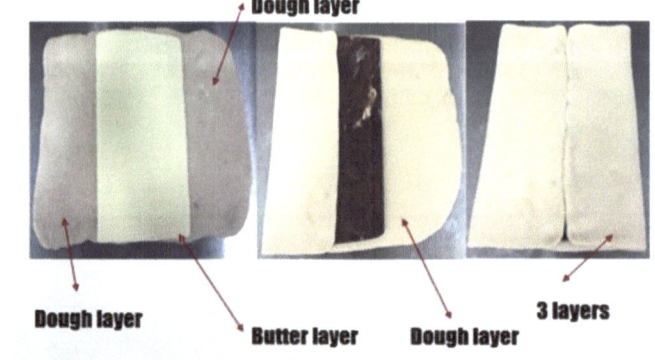

book, or it can be folded over the butter in the centre as seen in the diagram on the right, and the seam pinched closed. Below is an example of the sandwich method, where the dough's sides are cut to ease the elastic tension in the dough, exposing the butter on all four sides, just like a cheese sandwich appears between two layers of bread.

The following example explains how a lock-in **3**, followed by a 4-fold, determines the number of layers developed by lamination and emphasises the need to factor in the dough touching points. The photos and diagrams above illustrate the sandwich method of incorporating dough as a lock-in **3** to form the lock-in before sheeting. The pastry is first sheeted/rolled in the direction of the pinched seam reducing down in increments of 5 mm to 10 mm. Then the increments are reduced to 2 mm at a time to prevent tearing the pastry. The pastry is finally reduced to a thickness of 4 mm and folded into a 4-fold, which is offset to one side (4 mm × 4 folds = 16 mm pastry block height).

The 4-Fold or Book Turn

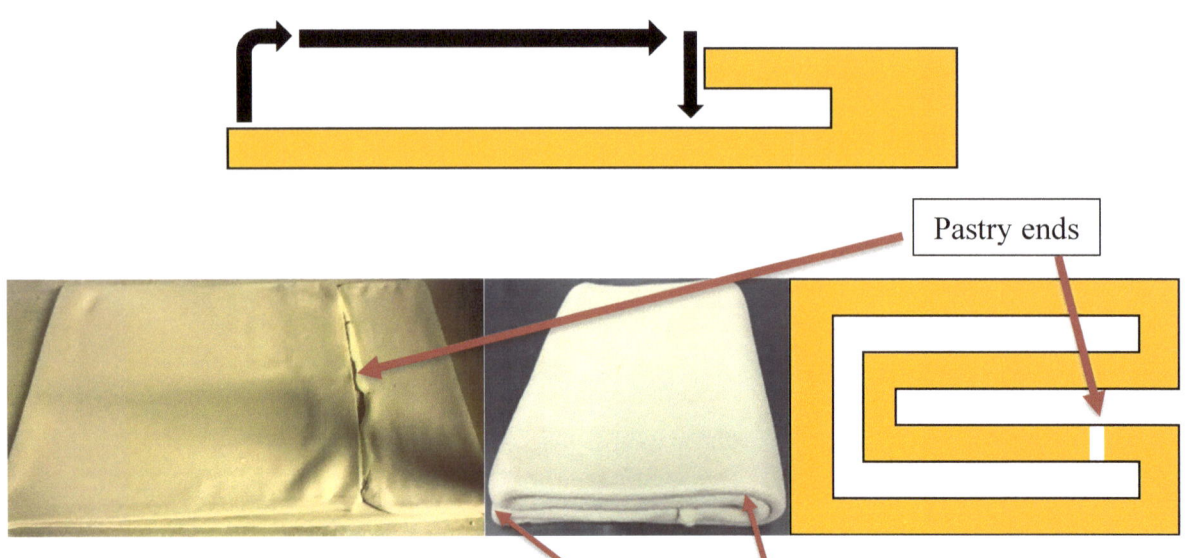

Note that the offset 4-fold will always have **open** and **closed** ends (or belly/bellies) of the pastry block. During folding and sheeting, the shaded areas/the dough touching points compress and form one dough layer, as illustrated in the diagram below. Therefore, the need to subtract one layer for each dough touching point to calculate the actual layers of alternating butter and dough.

	Dough	1
	Butter	2
Dough touching points	Dough	3
	Dough	3 (-1)
	Butter	4
Dough touching points	Dough	5
	Dough	3 (-1)
	Butter	6
Dough touching points	Dough	7
	Dough	3 (-1)
	Butter	8
	Dough	9

The dough is rotated 90° after the 4-fold, the belly is sliced with a knife (page 60) to release the elastic tension, and the same slicing on the other two folds at the open end of the pastry block. The dough is always rolled L-R with the belly of the dough facing the pastry maker (belly to belly will remind the pastry maker which way to orient the pastry when sheeting it).

The 3-Fold

The 9 layers formed so far in the process are sheeted out once more to 5 mm and then given a 3-fold-3 × 9 = 27 (-2 DTP) = 25 Layers, illustrated by photos and diagram below. The pastry block will be approximately 15 mm thick (3-fold × 5 mm thick = 15 mm).

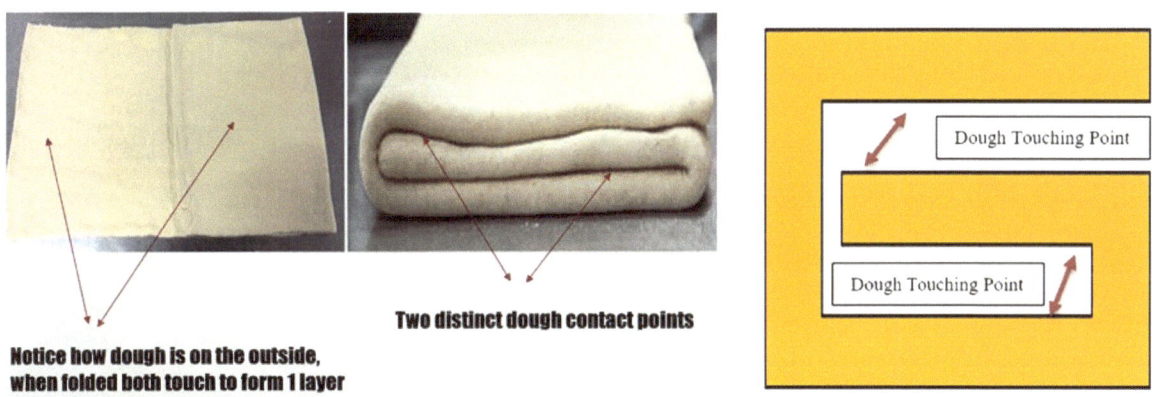

The pastry block now has 25 alternating layers of dough and butter. It should be pinned out to between 12 mm–15 mm, wrapped in plastic and chilled for 30 minutes –45 minutes in a freezer or between ice blankets to relax the gluten and control the pastry's temperature, arresting the fermentation.

Pastry Sheeter Settings

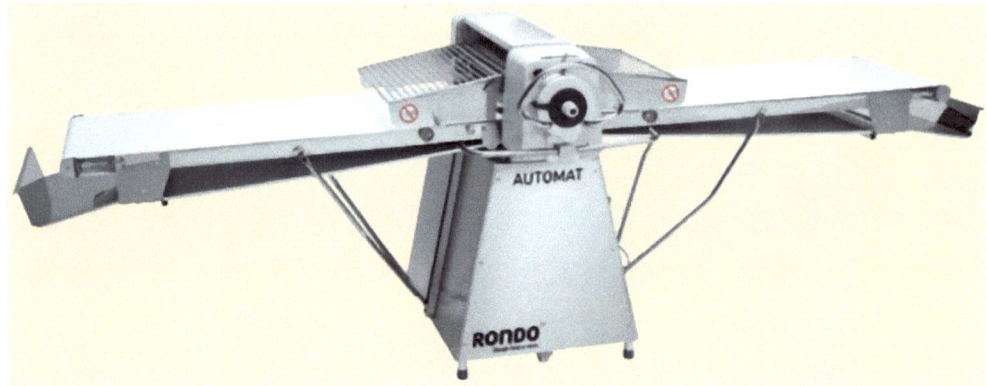

I have used Rondo Pastry sheeters worldwide to make the laminated pastry. I find them to be excellent machines. All sheeters sheet the dough or pastry down to a specific thickness on each fold sequence using a reduction wheel calibrated numerically in millimetres from 30 mm down to 1 mm. Larger machines have 45 mm or more comprehensive settings, but usually, it will be the smaller numbers that are mostly in general use. There is normally a locking adjustment to pre-set the rollers to a gap in mm. When using this function, the pastry will remain at the pre-set thickness programmed into the sheeter setting. It will not sheet any thinner, both preventing the operator sheeting too thinly and giving the pastry a predetermined sheeting thickness for consistency of lamination thickness.

Pre-Lock-In 3-4-3 Pastry Height Discussion

I recommend a starting point and to practice the **3**-4-3 system to begin pastry production, and when you become familiar, you can try other lamination systems of different numbering systems. The pastry can also be hand-laminated at all stages of production. If you are using a sheeter, sheet the dough to approximately 12 mm and the butter to 5 mm. When the lock-in is made, the dough block will have two dough layers of 12 mm, and one of butter of 5 mm thick–29 mm in height, which will easily pass through the 30 mm sheeter rollers. When hand rolling croissant dough, the pastry's height is not such an issue for initial sheeting height. Most basic reversible pastry sheeters have rollers that only open out to 30 mm, but bigger high capacity sheeters, as previously mentioned, open to 45 mm.

Lock-In and First 4-Fold Sheeting Settings Overview

My advised sheeter settings for sheeting the lock-in are as follows: The block of pastry should be prepared as the sandwich method, reduced gradually, descending in units of 5mm to 10 mm, then smaller increments of 2 mm from 10 mm downwards as the pastry gets thinner.

The stop button

Ensure the stop button has been engaged to prevent the pastry from being pinned too thinly. Use dusting flour sparingly.

- 30 mm
- 25 mm
- 20 mm
- 15 mm
- 10 mm
- 8 mm; then 6 mm
- 4 mm then fold as required (4)

Reducing the pastry block to 4mm ensures that the butter is correctly incorporated between the two dough layers. The pastry should be given a 4-fold at this stage. For example, if we give the pastry a 4-fold, the pastry block will be a little over 16 mm (4 mm thick × 4 folds) = 16 mm, plus the air spaces between. Reset the sheeter to 20 mm, rotate the pastry 90° to have the open end facing away from you and the closed-end (the belly) facing your stomach. Make sure to cut right through the pastry bellies to release the elastic tension before sheeting once more.

The 3- Fold Sheeting Settings

The pastry block has a 4-fold or book fold, should be approximately 16 mm, hence the setting of 20 mm, allowing for some expansion/relaxation. The pastry block should be reduced through the rollers as follows, descending in units of 5 mm to 10 mm. Then reduce by 2 mm increments; the final sheeter setting should be 5 mm as the butter is already well incorporated into the pastry.

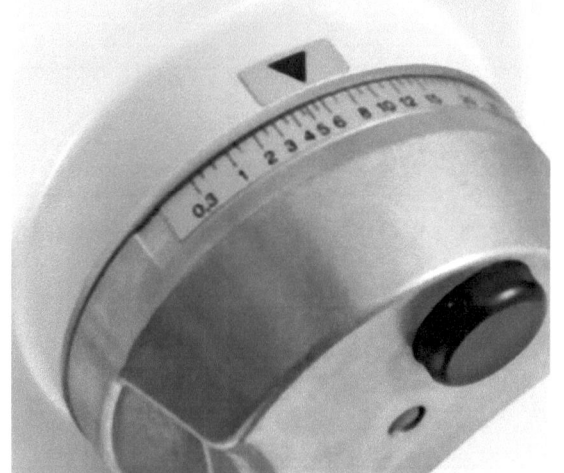

- 20 mm
- 15 mm
- 10 mm
- 8 mm; 6 mm
- 5 mm then fold as required (3)

The pastry should be given a 3-fold at this stage. For example, if we give the pastry a 3-fold, the pastry block will be a little over 15 mm high (5mm thick × 3 folds) = 15mm, plus the air spaces between. Reset the sheeter to 20 mm thick, rotate the pastry 90° to have the open end facing away from you and the closed-end (the belly) facing your stomach. Reduce in increments to 12 mm and chill in the freezer wrapped in plastic. Rest for 30 minutes –40 minutes before sheeting, then the pastry is now ready for final sheeting, cutting and shaping.

Final Sheeting Settings 3-4-3

The pastry block should now be a little more than 12 mm after relaxing in the refrigerator, hence the setting of 15 mm to commence sheeting, allowing for dough relaxation/fermentation. Cut the bellies (page 60); the pastry should be reduced as follows, descending in units of 5 mm to 10 mm. Then reduce the pastry sheet carefully down in increments of 2 mm at a time until you arrive at your final setting. The final sheeter setting or mm thickness should be set on the stop feature on the sheeter in advance, and the pastry sheeted to whatever thickness is required for your pastries. Once more, ensure the setting lock is on to prevent pinning the pastry too thinly.

- 15 mm
- 10 mm
- 8 mm
- 6 mm
- 4 mm- 3.5 mm for croissant or whatever thickness is required for an individual pastry.

Cutting The Belly Of The Pastry to Ease Elastic Recoil

In the picture above, I use a sharp knife to cut right through the pastry block's belly or folded part of the pastry block to ease the tension/elastic recoil in the pastry block just before sheeting it. Cutting keeps the pastry in a straight rectangle when processing. There will be two bellys in a 3-fold, two bellies in a 5 lock-in; (see page 61) and three bellies to cut in a 4-fold. Remember to always cut the pastry just before sheeting, folding and final sheeting.

Lesson #2 The 5-4-3 System

Pros and Cons of Pastry Made with This System

The pastry block has 49 layers, is less flaky externally, has a closer leafy honeycomb texture, is slightly more difficult to hand laminate due to developed elasticity from creating extra layers. Has good eating qualities, not as flaky as other pastry-making systems **3**-4-3 or **3**-4-4.

Process Method 5-4-3

The **5**-4-3 system begins by sheeting the chilled dough into a rectangle. The chilled, prepared butter block is then placed over 4/5ths of the dough; the dough is then folded into three, forming two layers of butter and three layers of dough-5 layers. In total, this is known as lock-in **5,** where the butter is locked into the dough.

The 5 Lock-In

- The first stage is always known as the "Lock-in" stage
- To fold a lock-in **5,** apply butter over the top 4/5ths of the pinned dough
- Stretch the dough flap at the bottom to cover 1/2 of the butter block
- Fold the top 1/3rd down, and you will have 5 alternating layers, 3 of dough, two of butter.

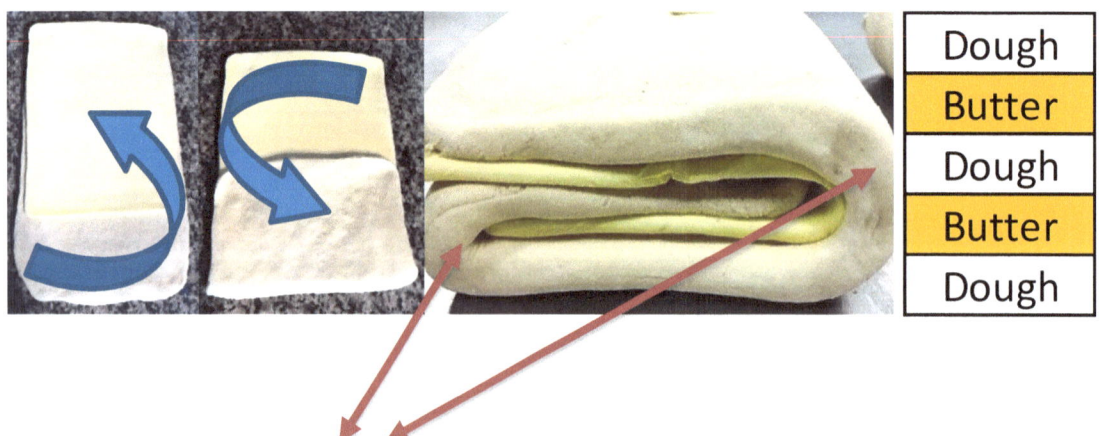

In this 5-fold, there are two **"bellies"** of dough. These should be cut through with a sharp knife (page 60) to release the dough's tension. The dough is then flattened out using a rolling pin. The pastry is reduced through the sheeter descending in units of 5 mm to 10 mm, then by 2 mm increments to 4 mm thick using a sheeter or a rolling pin to create a long even strip of pastry which will then be folded into a 4 or a book fold (4 mm thick pastry × 4 folds = 16 mm pastry block). If hand laminating, it is very important to use a small amount of dusting flour when rolling and ensure that the pastry never sticks to the work surface. When using a sheeter, very little flour is required. The layering can be damaged if the pastry sticks to the table or sheeter, and the resulting pastry will not be of good quality or appearance.

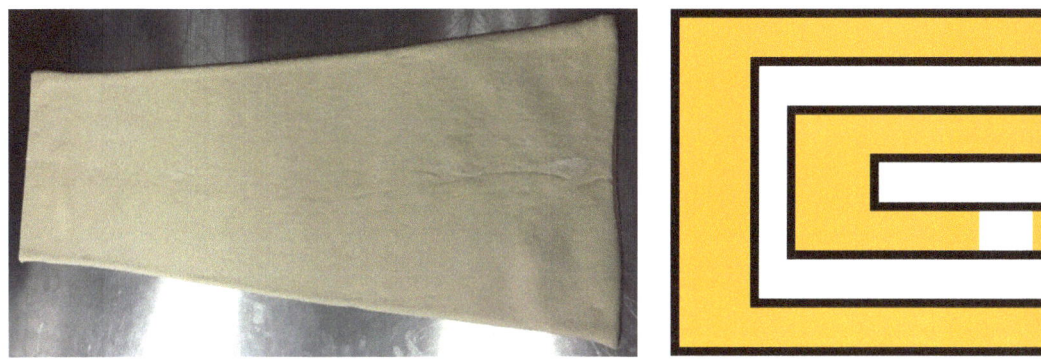

The 4-Fold

Following the lock-in **5**, the four-fold is the first of two folds after the lock-in 5, and after the pastry has been gradually sheeted in the direction of the seam to 5 mm thick, then given the four-fold or a 4. Remember to sheet L-R with the belly of the pastry facing yours! Follow the sheeting number guidelines given in the previous lesson on page 58.

Process Procedure The 4-fold

The pastry block is flattened and rolled or sheeted into a long, thin rectangle of approximately 4 mm. thick Pinning to this thickness helps ensure that the dough and butter are sheeted together to form a sheet of pastry with 5 distinct, separate layers and then given a book fold, also known as a (4), or a four-fold. This process is achieved by lifting the pastry's ends, drawing them together, and joining them slightly off centre. The pastry is then folded over like a book, and the pastry has been folded into 4 pleats, as seen in the central photographs and diagrams on page 63. The five combined layers of dough and butter from the **5**-lock-in stage are folded into four pleats, giving the pastry block technically **5** × 4 layers.

The pastry block now has 20 (-3 DTP) -17 layers, subtracting one layer each place where the dough touches dough or DTP. There are alternate layers of dough and butter. The pastry block should be approximately 16 mm high (4 mm pastry × 4 folds = 16 mm height of pastry block). Then sheet the pastry block to between 12 mm –15 mm, wrap it in plastic to prevent skinning and place in the freezer for 30 minutes. Ice blankets may also be used to chill down the pastry. Remember, when you compress two layers of dough together, they merge to become one layer and should be subtracted to count the total quantity of layers. Don't forget to rotate the pastry 90° (belly to belly) before sheeting. Note the 3 DTP below in a 4-fold.

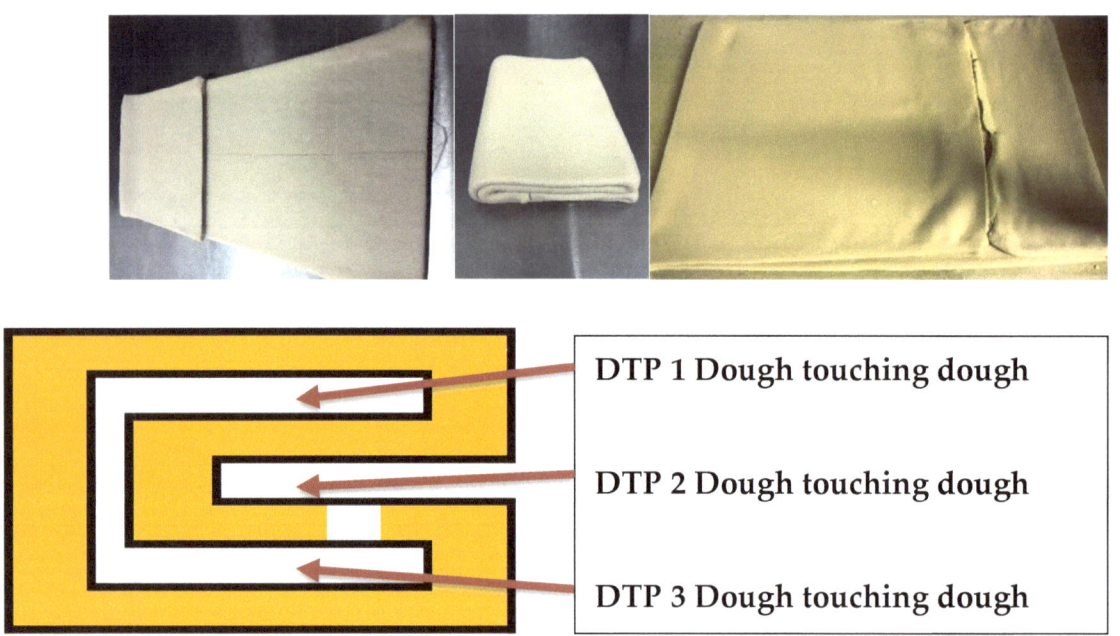

Freezing and Resting

The pastry should be sheeted to between 12 mm –15 mm and wrapped in plastic to prevent condensation and freezer burn. The reason for further sheeting is to thin out the pastry, so the freezer can reduce the core temperature of the pastry block quickly and prevent the yeast from fermenting before the pastry is prepared for final sheeting. When the pastry is folded in this manner above into a 4, there will always be two parts, the outside of the dough touching each or DTP. To calculate the number of layers in the pastry so far, where dough touches dough, it does not count as two separate layers. Remember, when you compress two layers of dough together, they merge to become one layer and should be subtracted in counting layers. Therefore, it is counted as one layer. This occurs three times in this 4-fold, three DTP are subtracted from the overall number of layers, and the pastry now has 17 layers at this stage in the process. See the diagrams below.

Layer Calculation Example After Subtraction Of DTP 4-Fold

		Layers		Layers
	Dough	1	Dough	1
	Butter	2	Butter	2
	Dough	3	Dough	3
	Butter	4	Butter	4
Dough touching points	Dough	5	Dough	5
	Dough	5 (-1)	Butter	6
	Butter	6	Dough	7
	Dough	7	Butter	8
	Butter	8	Dough	9
Dough touching points	Dough	9	Butter	10
	Dough	5 (-1)	Dough	11
	Butter	10	Butter	12
	Dough	11	Dough	13
	Butter	12	Butter	14
Dough touching points	Dough	13	Dough	15
	Dough	5 (-1)	Butter	16
	Butter	14	Dough	17
	Dough	15		
	Butter	16		
	Dough	17		

The 3-Fold

The croissant pastry is removed from the freezer and placed on the pastry sheeter. The pastry is then rolled to 5 mm into a rectangle and folded into a trifold, a simple fold or a 3. The pastry is now 15 mm thick. The dough has 17 × 3 layers—51 (-2 layers) where dough touches the dough in this production stage. The pastry now has 49 separate layers of dough and butter. Wrap well in plastic to prevent skinning and place in the refrigerator/freezer for 40 –60 minutes, or use ice blankets to chill down the pastry for 30 –45 minutes before sheeting.

 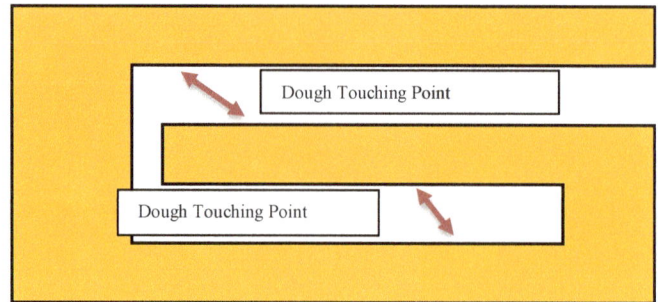

The Final Stage Is The Sheeting Stage

Sheeting effectively is the process of reducing the pastry to the thickness required for final processing. Sheet the pastry to between 3.5 mm –4 mm and place in freezer for 15 minutes. It helps prevent the pastry from shrinking. Process as you desire: croissant, pain au, chocolat, etc.

Lesson #3 The 3-4-4 System

Used generally for making Pain au Chocolat/Chocolatines, the 3-4-4 system produces 33 layers, and the chocolatines stand up better with the 8 layers than the 3-4-3 system used for croissant. As previously discussed, remember to cut the bellies of the dough with a knife each rotation of the pastry before sheeting and folding to ease the elastic recoil.

The Lock-in 3

The sheeting of the pastry block followed by folding sequences allows layers of dough and butter to build up simultaneously. As the butter is fat and the dough is water-based, they will remain separate when rolled out during the sheeting process. This allows for forming individual layers of dough and butter by folding the pastry in designated sequences. Following the **3** lock-in, the dough now contains three layers, i.e. dough, butter, dough. This is known as the first **3** of the lamination sequences. The pastry is placed on a sheeter and rotated 90° from the lock-in formation; the seam formed oriented to point horizontally towards the machine rollers. Cut the bellies (page 60). Commence sheeting, the thickness of the pastry is gradually reduced by 5 mm at a time to 10 mm. Then reduced in 2 mm increments to a final thickness of 4 mm for the lock-in on a pastry sheeter.

The 1st 4-fold

The pastry should then be given a book fold or a 4–fold, as illustrated in the photos below. It is vital the butter flows within the dough without breaking.

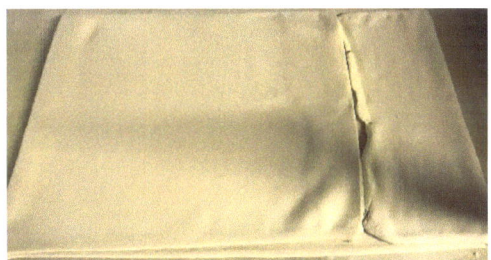 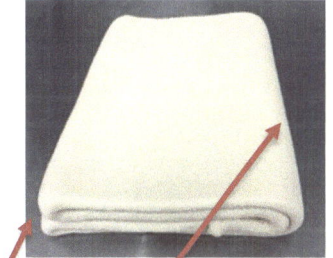

An offset 4-fold method is used here, noting the **open** and **closed** ends of the pastry block. An offset method of folding is recommended, as this reduces the possibility of a bulge in the leading edge of the pastry block, resulting in uneven sheeting. The mechanical friction of the rolling process generates heat and increases the temperature of the pastry. At this stage, it is recommended that the pastry is rotated 90° with the closed seam or belly facing the operator and reduced to a 12 mm thickness on the pastry sheeter, wrapped in plastic and placed in a freezer at -18 °C for 20 minutes. The 90° rotation of the pastry ensures that the pastry is stretched in each direction evenly throughout the process (NIIR Board of Consultants and

Engineers, 2014), which eliminates shrinkage in the final proofing and baking stages of production. Reducing the pastry to a thickness of 12 mm –15 mm enables the freezer to rapidly reduce the pastry's core temperature, controlling the fermentation until the proofing stage. Be sure to cut the pastry's bellies (page 60) to ease the dough's elastic recoil tension when sheeting it thin at the start of the next stage. As the pastry at lock-in initially had three layers or a **3**, it was sheeted and folded into four or a 4-fold. One would imagine that 3×4 would equal 12 layers; however, where dough touches dough in the folding process, known as The Dough Touching Point, Dough Touching point or DTP, one layer is subtracted at each dough touching point. Under compression, the dough merges to form a single dough layer while the butter layer remains unchanged. In the case of a 4-fold, three dough touching points are counted, leaving a total of 9 layers of dough and butter. The chilled pastry is then removed from the freezer after 40 minutes for the next stage of the process.

The 2nd and Final Fold In The 3-4-4 System

Once again, it is essential to rotate the pastry 90° to face the closed seam or belly facing the operator. The bellies of the pastry are cut (page 60), and the pastry block is then reduced in 5 mm increments to 10 mm, then it is reduced in 2 mm increments and sheeted to a thickness of 5 mm and given a second book-fold or a 4 as illustrated on the previous page. At this stage of the process, the pastry contains 9×4 layers or 36 layers. However, as there are three DTPs in a 4-fold, as seen on page 63, three layers are subtracted from the total, and the finished pastry now has a final total of 33 separate alternating layers of dough and butter. Rest for 40 minutes in the freezer. The pastry should again be rotated 90°, with the closed end facing the operator, sheeted to a thickness of 12 mm, wrapped in plastic and chilled in a freezer at -18 °C for 40 minutes –60 minutes to recover and relax the gluten.

The Sheeting Process

Remember to cut the pastry just before sheeting. Reduce the thickness gradually. It is now ready to prepare many different viennoiserie types, such as classic croissant, pain au chocolat or pain aux raisins and can be sheeted down to the required thickness.

Lesson #4 the 3-3-3 / 3 system

Pros And Cons Of Pastry Made With This System:

55 layers, less flaky externally than previous systems, closer honeycomb internal texture and good eating qualities, the most elastic of the doughs due to the extra layering, the pastry will shrink when cutting if not well-rested before sheeting. Takes longer to make because of the additional layers and the additional rest time required in the process.

Lock-in 3

The lock-in process is as in previous pastry making systems, all of which have been well described. I have included additional notes for using and handling coloured or flavoured types of butter. The second photo below has chocolate butter, butter made with 10% –15% cocoa powder in it, and the butter should be fully enclosed in the pastry to keep the dough sheeter clean.

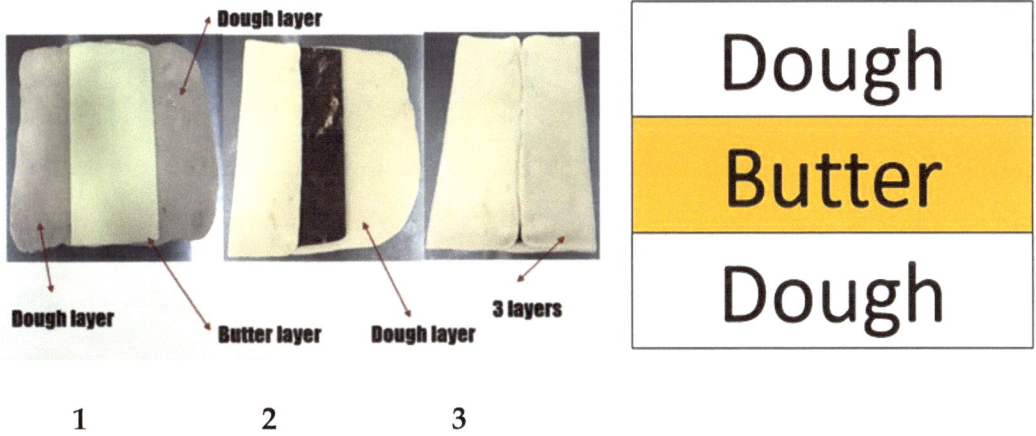

The 3-3-3 / 3 system begins by sheeting the chilled dough to a rectangle. The dough rectangle is placed on the table in landscape format. The pre-chilled prepared butter block is positioned in the middle of the dough. Imagine, for example, like the Irish flag, the dough rectangle is presented in landscape form. The butter block is placed in the middle of the dough rectangle. Next, the dough is folded over the butter to the centre. The two edges of the dough are pressed together in the centre, as shown below. There are now 2 layers of dough and 1 layer of butter - the 3 layers in total.

The Lock-In 3 Using Coloured Butter

#1   #2   #3

Note: In the photos above, the ends are sealed on the #1 dough on the left, as chocolate butter is inside. Sealing the butter entirely inside the dough protects the belts on the pastry sheeter from being soiled by the chocolate butter. If making plain croissant pastry, the ends should not be sealed as in #3 above. Alternatively, the sides can be cut with a sharp knife or pizza wheel and exposed, known as the *Sandwich Method* (see below), ensuring that no large masses of dough are present in the finished pastry and that the butter is evenly distributed between the formed layers.

The Lock-in and First 3-Fold (3-3)

The pastry block has the butter exposed on all sides. The pastry is rolled into a rectangle 4 mm thick and given a trifold, or a **3**. The pastry now has 3 × 3 = 9 layers (-2 DTP) or 7 separate dough and butter layers.

The Second 3-Fold (3-3-3)

The pastry is sheeted a second time to 5 mm given another trifold or 3. The folded pastry now has 3 × 7 = 21 layers (-2 DTP) or 19 alternating pastry layers. The pastry block should be rolled down to 12 mm –15 mm. Wrapped in plastic and placed in the freezer for 30 minutes –60 minutes or use ice blankets for 30 minutes –45 minutes.

The Third And Final 3-Fold (3-3-3 / 3)

The pastry is then taken from the freezer, rolled to 5 mm into a long rectangle, and folded into 3. Reduce the block to 12 mm –15 mm. The pastry now has 3 × 19 layers = 57 (-2 DTP) or 55 layers. The 12 mm –15 mm thickness of the pastry block helps achieve a low core temperature in the freezer swiftly. The pastry can now be either processed or frozen for up to two weeks at -18 °C at this stage. Seal in plastic and freeze to -18 °C. When required, remove the frozen pastry block and place it in a refrigerator at 3 °C –4 °C the evening before you need it to defrost overnight in the refrigerator. Then sheet the pastry the following morning, cut, proof and bake. If processing the pastry straight away, sheet the pastry to 3.5 mm –4 mm and place in freezer for 10 minutes –15 minutes, use at 2 °C –5 °C, which prevents shrinking the pastry. Process as you desire, croissant, pain au chocolat, or other varieties. **Tip:** You will find that you have much more control over the pastry's shape when it is well chilled, and the pastry will not distort as easily when handled at a cool temperature. If processing a lot of pastry together, leave half of it in the refrigerator/freezer as you work off the other half.

Overview of the 3-3-3-3 System, Lock-In, Sheeting and First Trifold

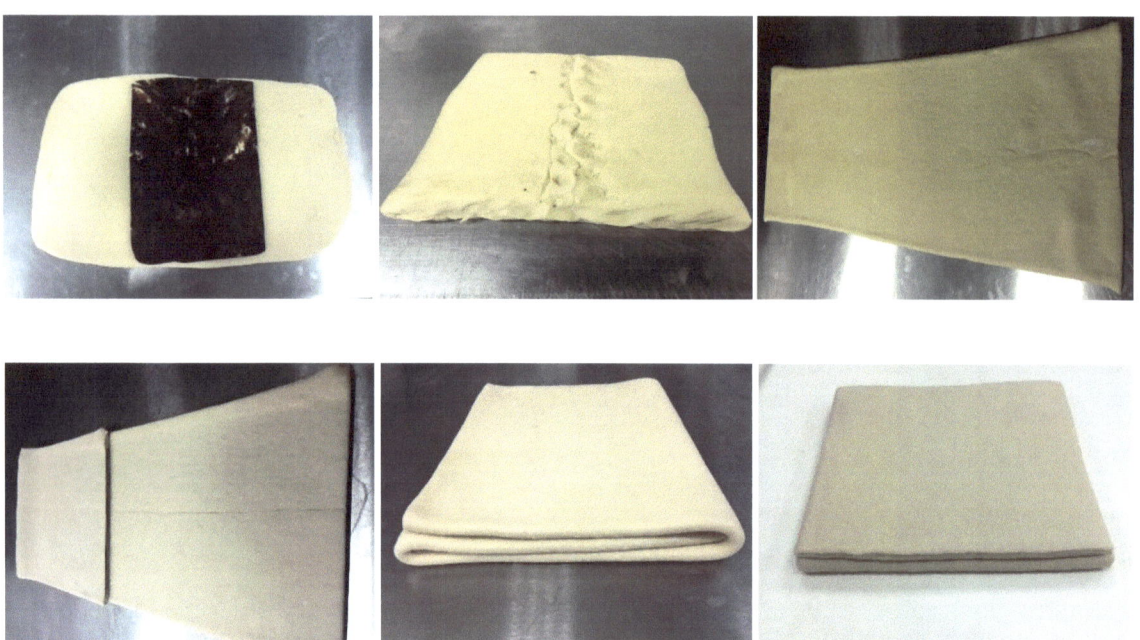

Recap lock in and first trifold There are many pastry folding combinations; I have just covered four systems here, three involving three folds (lock-in is the 1st fold) **3**-4-3; **3**-4-4 and **5**-4-3, the other with four folds **3**-3-3-3. Here's an overview of what has been covered and a mention of other systems. The lock-in number will always be the first number. The optimum thickness per layer is 0.08 mm-0.10 mm. Applying this formula to the layer sequences below, the sheeting thickness can be calculated using a thickness size of 0.08 mm per layer.

The Lock In 5 Series of Layering

Lamination system	Layers	Sheeting Thickness (Layers X 0.08mm)	Product type
5-4-4	65	5.20 mm	Single piece cut pastry
5-5-3	61	4.88 mm	Large Croissant
5-3-4	49	3.92 mm	Medium to large Croissant
5-4-3	49	3.92 mm	Medium to large Croissant
5-3-3	37	2.93 mm	Pain au Chocolat
5-5-2	41	3.36 mm	Medium Croissant

The Lock In 3 Series Of Layering

Lamination system	Layers	Sheeting Thickness (Layers X 0.08mm)	Product type
3-3-3-3	55	4.4 mm	Large Croissant
3-5-4	41	3.28 mm	Medium Croissant
3-4-5	41	3.28 mm	Medium Croissant
3-4-4	33	2.64 mm	Pain au Chocolat
3-4-3	25	2.0 mm	Large layered pastry
3-3-4	25	2.0 mm	Two merged dough 49 layers
3-3-3	19	1.52 mm	Outer layer for merged dough
3-4-2	18	1.44 mm	Twin lamination option 2 x 17 layers or 34 layers(-1 DTP) 33 layers

Processing Notes Recap for The Lamination 3-3-3 / -3

- Lock-in the butter as a **3** over the centre of the dough. Sheet to a thickness of 4 mm.
- Trifold #1 (3 layers) that we give the pastry also referred to as the second 3 in the sequence.
- Trifold #2 (3 layers) is given straight after the first; rotate the pastry block 90° to have the seam on the side. Sheet to 5 mm, fold and sheet again to 12 mm, wrap in plastic, place in the freezer.
- Trifold #3 (3 layers), sheet to 5 mm, rotate pastry block 90° to have the seam or belly facing you.
- The pastry is now made and needs time to recover from the sheeting.
- Sheet to 12 mm – 15 mm, wrap in plastic, place in freezer or place between ice blankets.
- When rested, sheet the pastry to 3.5 mm – 4 mm and chill again before cutting out for 5 minutes –10 minutes in the freezer.
- Ideally, leave the finished pastry for 40 minutes – 60 minutes in the freezer at -18 °C before final sheeting.

Keeping Count of The Number of Folds Made on The Pastry

A simple indentation made with your finger following each fold of the pastry will remind you what stage you are at in the pastry block production. This system also works well if there is more than one person in the bakery or pastry kitchen making the pastry together, on a production line, for example. The illustration above was made giving puff paste six single turns.

Recommended Layering for Different Pastry Sizes/Weight

Croissant: 5-4-3, 3-4-3 or 3-3-3-3; **Chocolatine:** 3-4-4

The more layers, the tighter the pastry will be. The smaller number of layers, the flakier the pastry will be. Remember, the yeast will rise the dough component of the pastry and generate lift in the oven. Larger sized pastries require a greater number of layers to support the increased mass.

Processing the Pastry - Rolling Out the Croissants

Calculating the final thickness of sheeting out the pastry can be measured and decided in advance by allowing an optimum thickness of 0.08 mm for each layer formed while making pastry. By counting the number of total layers formed when creating the pastry, for example, the 49 layers formed in the **5-4-3** system; or the 55 layers formed in the **3-3-3-3** system.

0.08 mm × 49 (layers from **5-4-3-** system) = Sheeting thickness of 3.92 mm

0.08 mm × 55 (layers from **3-3-3-3**-system) = Sheeting thickness of 4.40 mm

➢ Sheet to between 3.5 mm –4.4 mm or as required.
➢ Cut the pastry into triangles as in the photos below with a large French knife, or simply roll the end slightly thinner to elongate the croissant base of the triangles in the freezer for 10 minutes –15 minutes to arrest fermentation and prevent shrinkage.
➢ Make an incision in the middle of the base of the triangle 1.5 cm.
➢ Each piece should weigh between 65 g –75 g.
➢ The croissants should be slightly stretched to resemble the Eiffel Tower in shape.
➢ They can also be rolled on the base with a thin rolling pin to make the foot wider.
➢ Roll out gently, not tight, from the bottom in an outward motion.
➢ The croissant should freely open if held at the top and released.
➢ You may need to chill them once they are cut if they appear to be shrinking.
➢ If this is the case, chill them for 15minutes –20 minutes in the freezer at -18 °C.

Croissant and Chocolatine Cutting Guide Table

All measurements are a personal choice. Some people prefer to work with very long triangles. Others like fewer coils/shoulders or feet for their croissant. The guide on the next page will help produce a variety of sizes pastries from large to mini for breakfast buffets. All measurements are a guide. Lengths may be increased as desired. Croissant triangle ratio of 1: 3; Pain au Chocolat rectangle ratio of 1: 1.5 . Refer to the cutting size ratios for croissant and pain au chocolat below to ensure you cut your pastry into the correct sizes.

Croissant measurements		Triangle ratio 1 : 3	
	Width cm	Length cm	Thickness mm
Large	10	30	3.5 - 4
	9	27	3.5 - 4
Medium	8	24	3.5 - 4
Medium	7	21	3.5 - 4
	6	18	3.5 - 4
Small	5	15	3.5 - 4
Chocolatine measurements		Rectangle ratio 1 : 1.5	
	Width cm	Length cm	Thickness mm
Large	10	15	3.5 - 4
	9	13.5	3.5 - 4
Medium	8	12	3.5 - 4
Medium	7	10.5	3.5 - 4
	6	9	3.5 - 4
Small	5	7.5	3.5 - 4

Egg Washing and Proofing

Egg Wash Recipe

Two eggs

One egg yolk

Pinch of salt

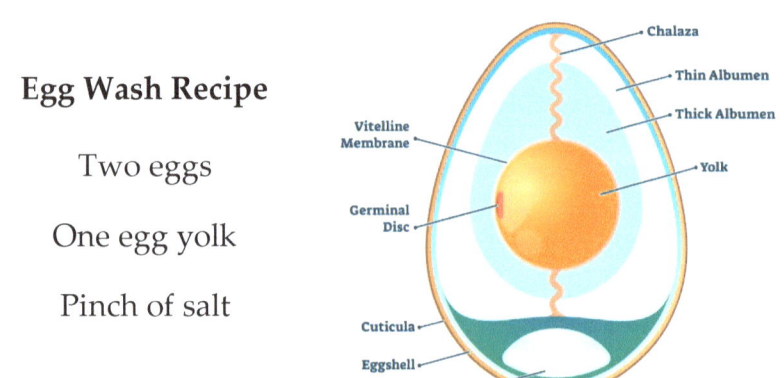

The addition of salt to the egg wash helps to breakdown the chalazae, which hold the yolk in place in the egg; giving a more homogeneous mix and uniform egg wash with no lumps of tissue in the wash.

- Proof at 26 °C –27 °C with 75% –80% relative humidity. It is important not to proof any hotter as the butter layers will melt and run out of the dough if the temperature exceeds 28 °C.
- Proofing time will always depend on temperature, amount of yeast and humidity.
- Proof time 1.5 hours –2 hours +. You will know they are proofed when the layers visually begin to separate. Also, the "Wobble Test" by shaking the tray gently, the proofed croissants should wobble like jelly.
- When egg washing pastry, use a very soft artist's paintbrush to apply the egg wash, taking care not to deflate the pastry when brushing.
- Always take care not to brush the cut edges of the pastry with egg, reducing its final volume.

Baking Temperature Factors

- Having the oven at the correct working temperature is essential.
- The preferred oven type for pastry is a fan or convection oven. However, using a deck oven requires a slightly hotter baking temperature setting of 200 °C with a heat intensity setting of 6 on top, 6 on the bottom and 6 at the door. The oven should be 10 °C –20 °C hotter before loading, and the temperature reset after filling the oven with product and trays.
- The fan oven should be set at 220 °C to allow a temperature drop of approximately 50 °C during the oven loading before baking.
- After loading the fan oven, drop the temperature to between 170 °C –175 °C depending on the oven type and the pastry's size, as each oven has its individual characteristics. The pastries should be egg washed and allowed to stand for 10 minutes to allow the egg soak into the outside, then baked for 14 minutes –20 minutes. A little steam can be added to the oven after loading but is not essential.

After Baking - Care of Pastry

- Allow the pastries to cool slightly on the tray before moving them.
- Place them on a wire tray to allow the air to circulate around the bottom so they don't get wet and soggy.
- When cool, do not stack pastry items one on top of each other as they will collapse.
- Store in airtight containers if not on display for sale to extend their shelf life.

Section 2
Recipes and Techniques

1. The Almond Twice-Baked Croissant

To make these delicious twice-baked croissants, follow the recipe overleaf

2. Almond Cream Recipe

Leftover croissants can be made into almond croissants which is a great way of using up leftovers. Cream the butter and sugar with the almonds and flour until fluffy, add the egg over three additions. Leftover croissants are cut in half, the crumb brushed with rum syrup, piped with almond cream, and the top is piped with more almond cream, then dipped into almond flakes. The almond croissants are baked then for 15 –20 minutes at 180 °C, allowed to cool, and dredged in icing sugar. If dusted when still warm, the icing sugar will turn yellow and does not look as attractive.

- 500 g   Butter
- 70 g   Pastry flour
- 450 g   Egg
- 500 g   Castor sugar
- 500 g   Ground almonds
- 20 g   Almond essence

Method for Almond Cream

Cream butter, flour, sugar and almonds until fluffy. Add the egg and almond essence over three additions.

3. Rum Syrup Recipe

100 g sugar; 100 g water; boil, allow to cool, then add 10 g of red rum and brush into croissant crumb. Store in the refrigerator when not in use.

4. Twin Lamination Croissant and Chocolate Croissant Pastry

I was always fascinated by pastry since I was a child; I had a burning desire and curiosity to push my knowledge boundaries. My dear deceased father and mentor Anthony Griffin, RIP, introduced me to lamination and taught me pastry principles as a young man. He would never realise the effect of his influence and tuition in our small family bakery in Galway, Ireland, would have on my life and career as a baker. I knew that I needed to give myself time and immerse myself in an environment away from work to focus on my creativity. In 2016, that itch was scratched. I bit the bullet. I decided to enrol as a mature student in the one-year masters' degree level 9 program at the Dublin Institute of Technology, now named Technological University Dublin. The masters' degree was in Food Product Development and Culinary Innovation at the School of Culinary Arts and Food Technology. One of the many modules for completion was to develop a totally new product with market potential, something never made before. So, I came up with the idea of a twin laminated pastry.

I was always a big fan of world-class baker David Bedu, the iconic bicolour croissant's creator. We served as jury members together in Casablanca 2019 at the African Bakery Cup. I took his creation one step further. His iconic pastry was a block of croissant pastry with a chocolate brioche top; I decided to conduct my research into developing a twin laminated pastry with a laminated chocolate pastry merged with plain croissant pastry. My choice of project was because, while I adored the bicolour croissant aspect and appearance, I found that the outside layer of chocolate brioche used in bicolor croissant production made the pastry less flaky. For me, the flakier the pastry, the more I enjoy it. If it doesn't make a flaky mess on my plate when I'm eating it, I am not fully satisfied, as I love the crunchy mouthfeel and texture that is unique only to a well-made laminated pastry. I decided to turn my attention and investigate making a laminated chocolate pastry and merge it with standard croissant pastry, double the layers, double the enjoyment and the mess! That was my inspiration and vision for the twin laminated pastry, which I went on to produce for my masters' degree practical in innovative product production. I used the time to experiment and tried well over 100 combinations of pastry lamination. Still, I learned a lot from the studies and graduated with my MSc. with first-class honours. I also won the Stafford Lynch award as the student of the year 2016 with the highest academic marks.

5. Preparing Chocolate Flavoured Butter for Twin Lamination

The critical differences in twin laminated pastry over bicolor pastry are preparing two separate laminated pastry blocks merged together and then processed as one block of pastry. Chocolate butter is prepared by mixing cocoa and butter slowly together on a stand mixer with a cake beater. The butter and cocoa powder are mixed until combined to form chocolate butter. The butter is then made into a butter block and chilled down to 3 °C before lamination.

6. Base Recipes for Croissant Pastry Production

The base croissant recipe page 52 will successfully make the most delicious laminated pastry. Many variations can be made by altering the butter flavours with cocoa powder, instant coffee, raspberry powder, strawberry powder, orange and lemon rind and seaweed. Double the dough recipe, prepare two different kinds of butter, there are infinite choices, but these are my own findings.

7. Twin Lamination Pastry with Spelt or Strong Flour

Stage 1: Making two different types of classic laminated pastry from one dough

- ➢ Croissant pastry - where the butter is added, and the pastry is laminated
- ➢ Chocolate croissant pastry - chocolate butter is added, and the pastry is laminated.

Stage 2: 45 minutes of room temperature fermentation, followed by overnight fermentation in a refrigerator at 3 °C

Stage 3: Lamination process of layering the butter into the plain spelt croissant dough using various lamination techniques and sequences

Stage 4: Lamination process of layering the chocolate butter into the spelt croissant dough using various lamination techniques and sequences

Stage 4. Merging of the two types of pastry together

Stage 5. Lamination, cutting and formation of individual pastry pieces

Stage 6: Proofing of the products 90 –120 minutes at 25 °C –27 °C and 75% –80% RH

Stage 7: Baking of the products at 170 °C –175 °C for 15–20 minutes (rack oven); 200 °C (deck oven).

Process Method

Remove the croissant dough from the refrigerator and process as set out on the next page, adding the chocolate butter to one of the doughs at stage 1. Process as per stage 5 instructions on page 84. Both doughs require similar lamination numbers for the desired layer quantities.

Stage 1 - Dough #1 - The Plain Dough with Plain Butter 3-3-3

Chocolate Dough	Stages	Instructions 3-3-3-Lamination system – 19 layers
Lamination stages:	Stage 1	Lock in the chocolate butter using a "3", pin to 5–6 mm
	Stage 2	Make a trifold turn (3) layers pin to 7–8 mm
	Stage 3	Make a trifold turn (3) layers pin to 12 mm, freezer 30 min
	Stage 4	Pin dough and apply over the laminated plain croissant dough

Stage 2 - Dough #2 - The Plain Dough with Chocolate Butter 3-3-3

Plain Dough	Stages	Instructions 3-3-3 Lamination system – 19 layers
Lamination stages:	Stage 1	Lock in the Butter using a "3", pin to 5 mm
	Stage 2	Make a book turn (3) layers pin to 7–8 mm,
	Stage 3	Make a trifold turn (3) layers pin to 7–8 mm, - freezer 30 min
	Stage 4	Pin dough and apply under the laminated choc croissant

Stage #3 - Merge The Chocolate and Plain Doughs Together and Process As Below

Details Sheeting:	Stages	Instructions:
Sheeting the pastry:	Stage 5	Moisten the pastry using a spray bottle of water. Place chocolate dough on top of plain dough, sheet together
Thickness:		Pin pastry to 3.5–4.2 mm – chill in the freezer for 20–30 min
Shape:	Stage 6 Proofing Stage 7 baking	Mark with dividers and cut with a French knife Triangles 10 × 30 cm – Croissant Rectangles 8 × 14 cm – Pain chocolat
Final proof time:	90 – 120 min	Maximum of 27.5°C 85% humidity. Egg wash before baking
Baking temperature:	185°-200°C	
Baking time:	15 – 18 min.	

Mixing Stage Plain or Spelt Croissant Dough # 1

Stage	Ingredients	Kg/g.	Method
1	T55 or Spelt Flour Salt Butter	1010 20 32	Mix flour & salt together in a 10qt Hobart mixer. Use the dough hook attachment Add the butter
2	Milk fresh Water Sugar Milk powder Yeast Malt	258 258 121 26 66 2	Disperse yeast, dry milk powder and sugar in the water/milk. Use a hand whisk to blend and add all to stage 1. Mix the dough for 4 minutes on slow – 4 minutes on 2nd speed Mix ingredients to a stiff dough. Cover with plastic
	Total:	1793	Ferment at room temperature 45 minutes. Set aside in refrigerator overnight @ 3°C 12–18hrs
3	Butter Dry 84%	500	Prepare butter for lamination as demonstrated in the YouTube video. https://youtu.be/Cj0gEXtXexw
	Total:	2293	

Mixing Stage Plain or Spelt Croissant Dough and Chocolate Butter #2

Stage	Ingredients	Kg/g.	Method
1	T-55 or Spelt Flour Salt Butter	1010 20 32	Mix flour & salt together in a 10qt Hobart mixer. Use the dough hook attachment Add the butter
2	Milk fresh Water Sugar Milk powder Yeast Malt	268 268 121 26 66 2	Disperse yeast, dry milk and sugar in the water/milk. Use a hand whisk to blend and add all to stage 1. Mix the dough for 4 minutes on slow – 4 minutes on 2nd speed Mix ingredients to a stiff dough, Cover with plastic
	Total:	1793	Ferment at room temperature 45 min Set aside in refrigerator overnight @ 3 °C 12-18 hours
3	Butter 84% Cocoa	500 75	Prepare butter for lamination. Mix on a machine and prepare butter block as demonstrated in the YouTube video. https://youtu.be/Cj0gEXtXexw
	Total:	2368	

Examples Of Twin Laminated Dough and Makeup

When using two different types of laminated dough together, the optimum result was achieved by using the following combination of lamination sequences to both individually coloured doughs separately and then merging them both together:

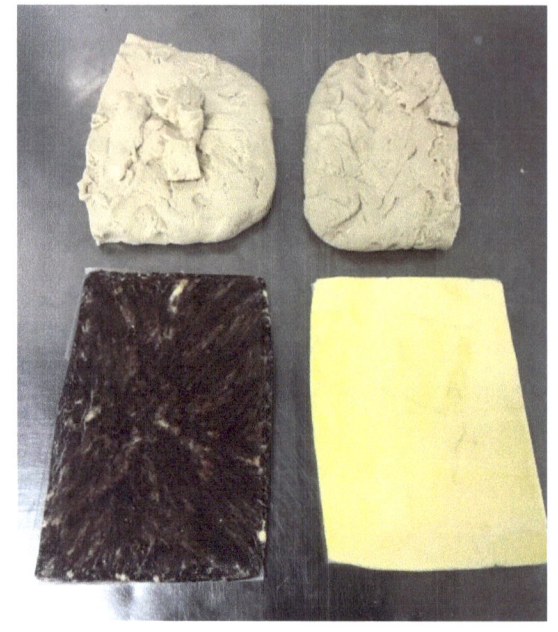

#1 using the – **3**-3-3 sequence of laminating for the white laminated dough (19 layers)

#2 using the – **3**-3-3 sequence of laminating for the laminated chocolate dough (19 layers) 19+19 =38 (-1 DTP) total 37 layers. My research into pastry has found that the combined sequences above give 37 layers of pastry and are the most appropriate systems for all types of twin merged laminated pastry. Remember to place the chocolate or coloured/flavoured dough face down on the table when cutting, then when processed, the coloured pastry will be on the outside of the combined pastry after processing.

           1   2   3   4

The sheeted doughs are measured, sprayed or brushed with a little water to make one surface sticky; then both are pressed together with a rolling pin to form one block of pastry. They should be gently rolled together on each side to ensure cohesion before sheeting. The pastry can then be sheeted and cut into various shapes, and fillings of choice such as chocolate bars and/or candied orange peel added. The next series of photos show the pastry marked and cut, rolled, orange peel addition, fully shaped and fully proofed.

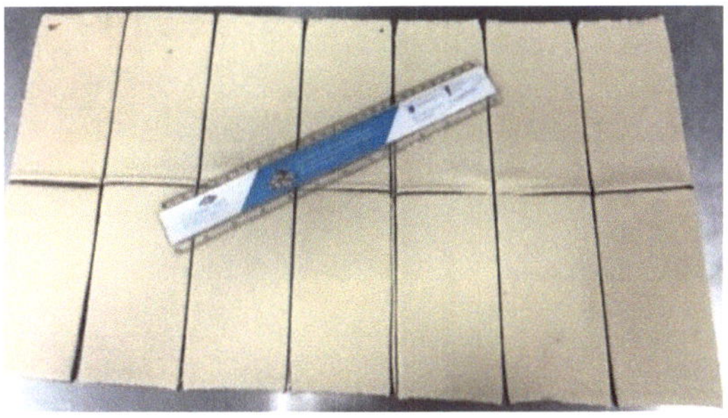

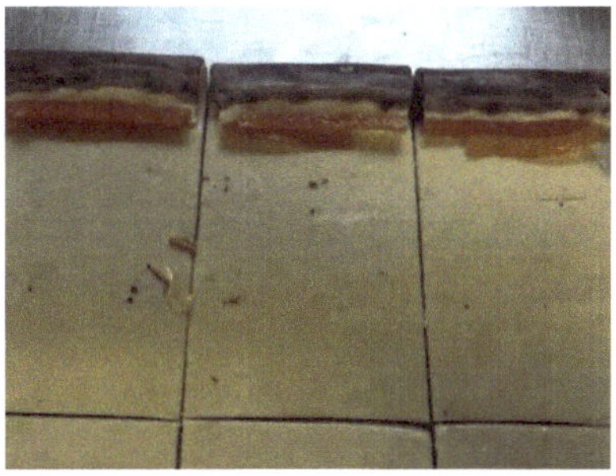

To ensure the pastry is fully/correctly proofed before baking, visual clues indicate when the pastry is ready to bake. The first visual clue is when air spaces appear between the pastry layers running right through the pastry from the outside to the core. Remember that the pastry's core is where the temperature takes the longest to be penetrated by the

proofer's heat. If not correctly proofed, the pastry will have a dense, gummy core. Viennoiserie will always proof from the outside to the centre. Coiled and high pastry such as croissant and pain au chocolat will always take at least 2 hours to proof under normal proof conditions (26 °C –27 °C). Coiled but flatter pastries, such as pain aux raisins, cinnamon rolls or those cut with cutters, such as the raspberry pear pastries, will proof faster as they are not as thick or high. Pay particular attention to the innermost fold, the start of your pain au chocolat coil in the very centre. If there is good separation as seen in the photo on the previous page and not gummy at the core, you are nearly there.

The "Wobble Test" is the other visual clue where, when the tray is gently shaken, the entire pastry quivers like a bowl of jelly. I attach a link on YouTube where this test may be viewed. Wobble Test: click the link - http://youtu.be/czyabhubp1k pain au chocolat "Wobble" Test (Griffin, 2016).

The photos above are examples of chocolate and plain merged laminated spelt dough. A YouTube video showing some of the above pastries being baked on time-lapse is available on the link below. Chocolatine baking in a time-lapse movie (Griffin, 2016).

Click the link for time-lapse video http://youtu.be/-yvqngzw3gs

8. The Double Chocolate Chocolatine

The double chocolate twin laminated pastry is a chocolatine, coiled style pastry made with two types of laminated croissant pastry, chocolate and plain butter pastry is made separately and then it is pinned together to a thickness of 3.5 mm, cut to 8 cm wide and 12 cm long. Two croissant bars are used inside the pastry, as is typical for chocolatine, and the pastry can be dusted with dark cocoa or icing sugar after cooling. To make an even crispier pastry, this one is typically scored several times before rolling. Scoring creates more surface area in the pastry. The layers open out during the proof stage and increase the surface area of crispy layers.

9. Bicolor Croissants and Pain Au Chocolat 3-4-4

My dear friend French master baker David Bedu, based in Florence, Italy, was the creator of the "Croissant Bicolor." He inspired me to both mimic and recreate his legendary croissant in a different and unique form. The croissant bicolor is the fusion of a croissant dough block before sheeting with a coloured sheet of brioche.

There have since been countless bicolour croissant variations, including strawberry, raspberry, coffee, purple or blue raspberry, green apple, to mention but a few. Chocolatines also look very pretty when made using bicolour pastry, especially when scored, as seen in the photo to the right.

To make a nice croissant bicolor chocolate, the white croissant pastry is laminated using the **3**-4-4 sequence. Chocolate brioche (made by taking 25% of the croissant dough and adding cocoa powder, butter, yeast and water, mixing it to a chocolate dough) is sheeted separately at a ratio of 4:1 dough weight or 225 g of chocolate yeasted brioche dough per kg of croissant dough. The brioche dough was coloured by the addition of dark cocoa powder at a rate of 10% flour at the mixing stage. This chocolate dough is then sheeted and placed on top of the plain croissant dough before final sheeting, and the combined dough and brioche is then reduced to 3.5 mm by passing it through the dough sheeter several times. In the chapter Coupe du Monde Chocolatine, I have a recipe for chocolate dough using the croissant dough you are making, and it saves time, not having to weigh a separate dough each time you make croissant bicolour (CDMC recipe page 123).

The diagram and photo above show the thin layer of dough applied to the pastry block for making bicolour products. Another popular colour for croissant bicolour is red. Many unique products can be made using a combination of bicolor croissant dough and the

addition of fillings and flavours that complement the chocolate as orange, mint and raspberry. When colouring brioche dough, I recommend using dry powder or edible paste colours, which should be added at the beginning of the mixing phase. Paste and powder colours retain most of their colour following the baking process. There are also many natural concentrated food colours for making this type of pastry on the market today. Dosage is roughly 1% of concentrated dry colour powder to dough weigh for powder coloured doughs. Cocoa powder used for chocolate bicolour should be Dutch non-acidic cocoa powder used in dosages of 10% –15 % of the dough weight. Acidic cocoa powder can cause the chocolate dough to separate and fall apart, ruining the bicolour aspect.

10. The Orange Chocolate Bicolor Chocolatine 5-4-3

The orange chocolate bicolor is made using 250 g of chocolate brioche per 1 kg of croissant dough. The dough is merged with the chocolate brioche and sheeted to 3.5 mm –4 mm. The pastry is cut 15 cm long × 8 cm wide with the chocolate brioche side of the pastry face down on the table. The chopped pieces are brushed with a minimal amount of orange oil and rolled up with two chocolate bars and a candied orange peel slice. The pastry is proofed and baked, allowed to cool and garnished with half a candied orange slice. Homemade chocolate bars can be used and infused with orange oil for extra flavour in the pastry. It is one of my all-time favourites. The orange/chocolate example above was made in Bordeaux, France, when I travelled there to Foricher Mills. I was hosted by my dear friend Yann Foricher who makes wonderful flours. This pastry was made using Foricher Gruau T-45 flour, and it produces spectacular pastry. I also used Lescure French butter in the pastry; the flavour and volume were amazing.

11. The Cross-Laminated Croissant and Chocolatine

Two-tone, three-tone or four-tone pastry can be made up using the techniques mentioned earlier. In the case of a cross-laminated single colour, for example, a chocolate croissant dough is made using coloured butter and a smaller number of layers the **3**-3-3 system. The pastry is then frozen in a block, and when semi-hard, it is sliced into strips, and the strips are placed facing up on top of a chilled plain croissant block of dough until the dough is entirely covered. The block of pastry is then sheeted, ensuring that the layers on the top of the block are stretched to elongate them and not widen the layers as this will lose the effect of cross lamination.

Examples of Cross Lamination Techniques

This example of cross lamination on the right was made using raspberry butter. 30 g of raspberry powder was added to 300 g of butter and beaten together on a kitchen aid. The raspberry butter was then taken out of the mixing bowl, and a butter block was made. The pastry was laminated 3-4-4, 12 mm thick, and cut in half. Set one half aside. From the other half, cut strips 10 mm thick and place them on the top of the other half of the pastry in straight lines to make the cross-lamination effect which is explained in the next section.

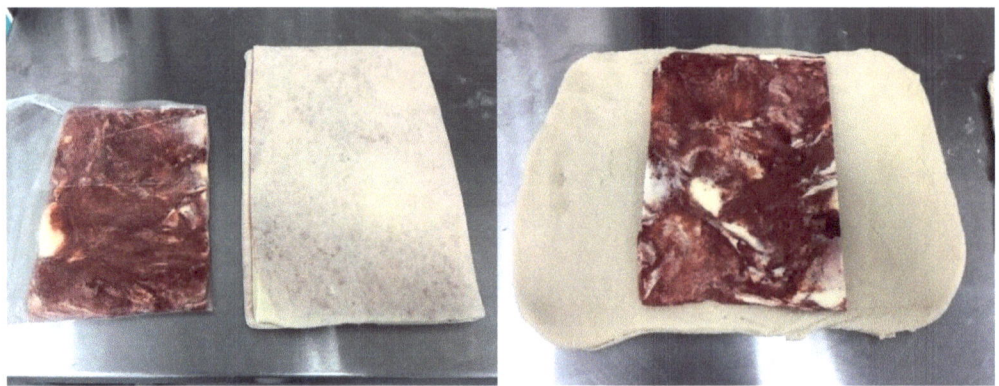

Using 10% freeze-dried fruit powders, flavoured butter can be made. Examples include vanilla, citron, raspberry, strawberry, blackberry, and mango. All add exceptional colour and flavour to the pastry. Simply add 10 g freeze-dried fruit powder per 100 g of lamination butter used in your recipes. Place in a stand mixer with a beater attachment, mix on slow to incorporate and make a normal butter block.

The coloured pastry dough is laminated 3-4 as separate doughs and then stacked together

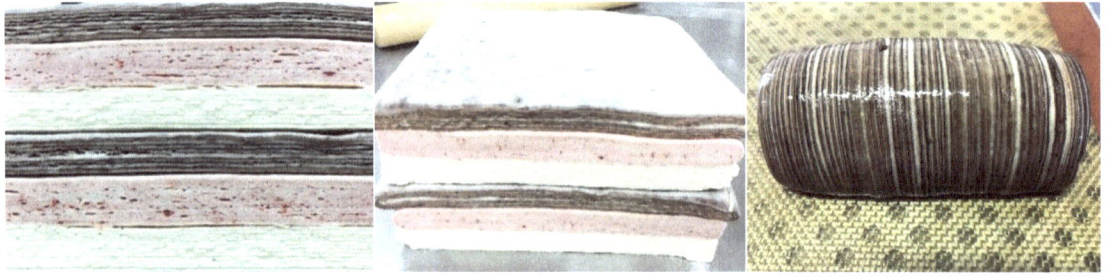

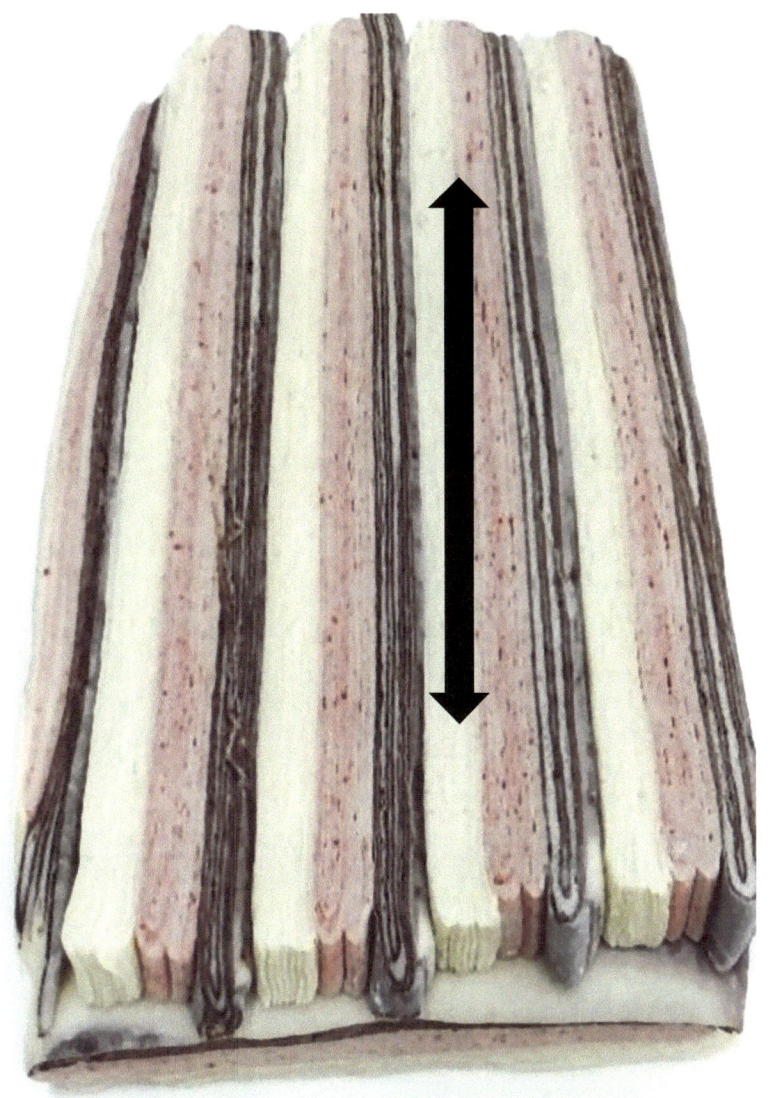

The three stacked colours are sheeted to 15 mm, cut in half and merged together. The pastry is then reduced to 12 mm and rested for half an hour in the freezer at -18 °C. Two-tone or three-tone pastry can be made up using the techniques mentioned earlier. The three pastry blocks are merged together as one block and frozen to a semi-solid state. Cut in half, wet and stack the frozen pastry halves on top of each other, sheet to 12 and slice into strips of 5 mm thick, which are placed onto a block of croissant dough facing up. The dough is then sheeted in the same direction as the cut, exposed, layers; taking care only to elongate the top layers and not widen them when sheeting the pastry. The pastry should be rolled in the direction of the black arrow, in the direction of and with the cut layers' flow, as seen above; otherwise, the layers will widen instead of elongating. The cross-lamination effect will be lost if care is not taken.

12. The Orange Chocolate Twin Laminated Chocolatine

Inspired by David Bedu, I developed this new concept in 2015/2016; twin-laminated pastry during my master's degree studies. The orange chocolate croissant is a pain au chocolat-type pastry made using two different laminated dough types merged together before the final sheeting. A plain croissant dough and also one made using chocolate butter. The plain croissant dough is laminated using the **3**-3-3 system, and the chocolate croissant dough is made using the **3**-3-3 laminating system. Both doughs are merged and sheeted to 4 mm, giving 37 layers. The pastry is placed on the worktable with the chocolate side down and then cut into rectangles 15 cm long × 8 cm wide. The pastry is brushed with a tiny amount of orange oil and a chocolate croissant bar. I also use candied orange peel strips to enhance the flavour. The candied orange slices are used to garnish the pastry when cool. The orange strips can be made at home. There are plenty of online resources, such as Epicurious, with step-by-step instructions to make them at home. https://www.epicurious.com/recipes/food/views/simple-candied-orange-peel-350798 also, slices are available commercially from Keylink Ltd in the UK (see page 162 & 163). The candied orange bars are a filling designed to enhance the flavour of the product. They are added before baking for flavouring purposes. They are a natural product, free of sulphides.

13. The Lye Dipped Croissant 3-3-3

Another interesting variation of the croissant is a lye/pretzel croissant. If used as a savoury item, adjustments to the recipe can be made by reducing the recipe's sugar levels by 80%. Lye is also known as Sodium Hydroxide (NaOH) and, as a baking application, is used to produce pretzels and lye rolls. Lye products are popular in Germany and across Europe. Lye croissants are another variant that may be explored as an option for a different pastry by bakers already using lye. The croissant is processed in the usual manner, and when 3/4 proofed, the croissants are placed into a freezer or a blast chiller for 10 –15 minutes until the outside is frozen solid and the product can be handled without collapsing. A 1:10 solution of reduced food-grade lye or NaOH is prepared while the croissants are in the freezer.

Using proper safety equipment to include safety goggles, plastic bib apron, and elbow-length rubber gloves, the frozen croissants are dipped into the lye, allowed to drip on a wire tray before being placed onto baking sheets lined with baking parchment. The croissants should be sprinkled with rock salt or shaved salt to distinguish them from other products. The lye croissants are then baked as normal, and the baking process removes the harmful lye through a chemical reaction between the heat of the oven and the NaOH. Lye croissants have a rich chestnut colour exposing the paler white layers of pastry in contrast to the lye's accelerated Maillard reaction on the outer skin. They are attractive to look at and make nice savoury canapes.

It is most important to wash all equipment and trays which comes in contact with lye, as the lye will stain clothing and is corrosive to metal. As lye is a known poison, it should be stored in a secure area when not in use. The dilutions used to make pretzels, or lye croissant should also be kept in a secure area in a clearly marked container as toxic if ingested. Always wear protective clothing such as a disposable plastic apron, gloves and safety glasses when handling lye.

14. Four Colour Cross Lamination-The Christmas Chocolatine

While working as a jury member in Shanghai, Coupe Louis Lesaffre, November 2019, I was inspired by all the international teams who had so much to contribute, especially team Japan, who produced a stunning three coloured, diamond-shaped viennoiserie. I used four colours in my own interpretation of this magnificent pastry. My pastry variation was made by colouring three separate doughs, red, green, pink, and plain dough, to create the four-colour Christmas coloured effect. I used bake-stable powdered colour used for macarons in each dough. The butter was not coloured. I used my recipe, page 52. I made a double recipe and divided the dough in half. The large plain dough was laminated **3-4-3** and then rested in the freezer for 35 minutes. Then I divided one dough into four and coloured the dough using food colour. Each of the coloured doughs was laminated **3-4** and stacked on top of each other, chilled for 30 minutes. Refer to the cross lamination instructions on pages 92 –94; before cutting in half, stacking one on top of the other to get double the layers for slicing. Then I carefully marked and cut the four-colour dough into 5 mm strips.

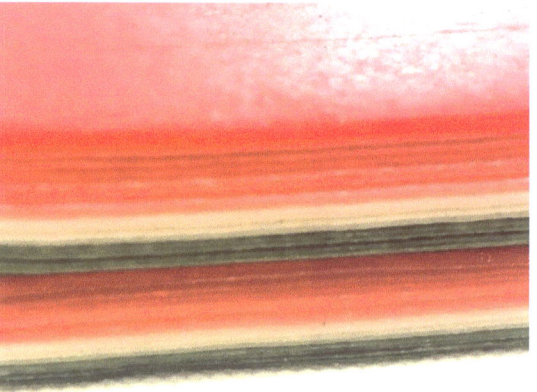

The multi-coloured cut layers are laid down on the plain dough facing upwards, neatly, and each layer is sprayed with water to help them stick together. The pastry is then sheeted, marked and cut to size.

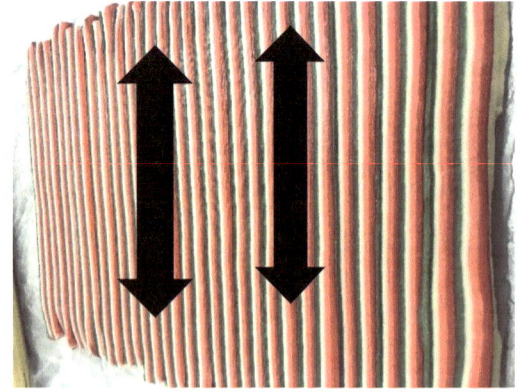

I cut croissant 10 cm wide × 30 cm long; Pain au Chocolate 8 cm wide × 15 cm long. The arrows above show the direction to sheet the cross-laminated pastry correctly before cutting. I sheeted to 4 mm thick. I made various chocolatines and croissants from them using chocolate bars, strawberry, and cherry fillings. I have included an instructional video on

YouTube on making your own home-made chocolate bars, and I used freeze-dried strawberry pieces in the chocolate bars to give the pastry some zing. Follow the link below to see the video making the strawberry chocolate bars. https://youtu.be/0wMbMnD5ZxY

Four-colour proofed chocolatine with vertical lines and an un-proofed croissant with horizontal lines above; the sheeted pastry's precise lines below and a chocolatine with horizontal lines.

15. Seaweed Croissant

Using the Noribake seaweed blend, I began researching the use of seaweed in bakery products and as a food supplement in 2015. I began my research by reviewing Japan's seaweed consumption (the highest, per capita, in the world, with the lowest incidence of obesity and cancer). I introduced new Irish seaweed baked products to customers and colleagues and examined how seaweed could be integrated more efficiently into the western diet. The western diet and food culture differ greatly from that of Asia. So different approaches are required to encourage greater consumption of seaweed which is high in naturally occurring iodine. Bread and baked products are consumed by most western countries. Adding dried seaweed to flour or in butter for baked goods or in health drinks are considered the most appropriate models for achieving this and indeed yielded encouraging results (Griffin, 2015: ii).

The addition of seaweed to croissant pastry can be achieved in many ways

- ➢ Added as a dough ingredient
- ➢ Added to the butter in advance of lamination
- ➢ Added in a filling after baking

I conducted many test bakes using a product named Noribake (now called Smart Bake), which is available in health food shops nationwide in Ireland, or by contacting the company via their FaceBook page of the same name. The dry seaweed tended to puncture the dough when directly incorporated into it, reducing the croissants' volume in a similar way that wholemeal bread does not yield the same volume as white bread when baking bread or pastry. Following many test bakes, the most beautiful and tasty croissants are made by blending the laminating butter with the seaweed one day before lamination and using a **3-4-3** system to process the croissants. Seaweed butter and seaweed croissant, as seen above, were developed during my 2014 –2015 research for my BSc. Honours degree.

As seaweed has a strong flavour, the quantity added to the lamination butter should be 60 g per kg of butter. The dried seaweed is simply mixed with the butter in a machine with a beater until blended, then a seaweed butter block is made by forming it into a butter block for lamination. The seaweed butter should be chilled before use, and the croissants are made up in the usual manner. The **5-4-3** laminating sequence also produces an excellent seaweed croissant which is delicious for seafood canapés when used with various seafood fillings such as prawn, crabmeat or smoked salmon.

16. Woodgrain Effect Croissant 3-4-3

Woodgrain effect croissants are made using a croissant dough block and two yeasted brioche doughs, one plain, one chocolate. The doughs are pinned out thin to a thickness of 3 mm -4 mm into a neat rectangular sheet. The dough can be sprayed with a fine mist of water, and the two doughs are stuck together and gently rolled with a rolling pin to ensure cohesiveness. The combined doughs of  chocolate and plain brioche are rolled up tightly together into a Swiss roll shape, wrapped tightly in parchment paper and frozen until solid.

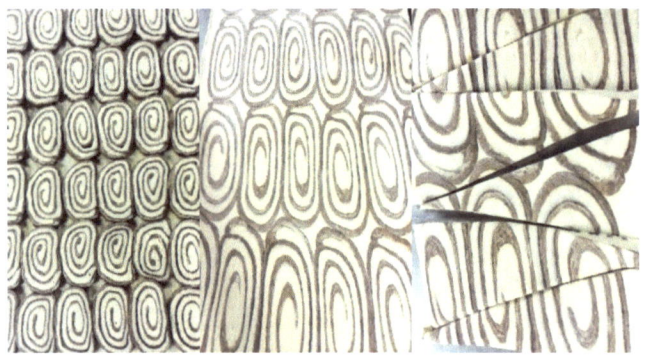

Woodgrain Croissant Effect Using Brioche Dough

A block of chilled pre-laminated croissant dough, which has yet to be sheeted out, is placed on the table and sprayed with a gentle mist of water to enable the brioche dough to stick to it effectively. The frozen brioche dough is then carefully cut into slices of 2 mm –3 mm thick discs and placed on top of the croissant pastry, ensuring proper alignment until all the pastry block is covered. The block is then rolled out as normal to produce croissant or pain au chocolat, as detailed earlier in the book.

Following the correct procedures for croissant and pain au chocolate, the pastries are shaped and proofed in the usual way as described above. The one difference recommended is that the pastry should be baked in a deck oven for 20 minutes at a temperature of 200 °C. The fan oven gives the pastry too much colour, and the distinction of the wood grain style pastry is not as effective when baked in a fan oven unless baked at a much lower temperature approximately.160 °C.

17. Frozen Pre-Proofed Croissants and Viennoiserie

Pre-proofed frozen croissant and viennoiserie production is the realm of the industrial baker. While I touch on the subject by way of a mention, the process is very scientific, requires expensive equipment /ingredients and uses a lot of energy in production and storage. The recipes supplied in this book can be adjusted to make the pre-proofed frozen pastry by making minor adjustments to the recipes and the process. Pre-proofed frozen pastries, by nature, require stiffer dough. This type of frozen pastry's hydration requires adjustment down to 50% of the flour weight. Special dough improvers and yeasts for the freezing process are available on the market. Lesaffre company make a suite of products specifically for this type of frozen production. The addition of dough improver for viennoiserie should be at a dosage recommended by the manufacturer but usually at 1% of the flour weight. A blast chiller is an essential component in producing pre-proofed frozen croissant dough because of the chiller's ability to rapidly reduce the pastry's core temperature. Blast freezing freezes the water in the pastry rapidly, keeping the ice crystals small, minimising the damage to the product texture and the yeast during the freezing process.

The dough making process is a no-time dough, lacking in overnight fermentation to generate flavour, so the addition of up to 20% sourdough to the recipe will add flavour to viennoiserie made in this manner. However, adjustments to the recipe are required to balance all the variables, including the quantity of butter used in the final dough. The dough is processed as a no-time dough with a target dough temperature of 20 °C is desirable. The mixed dough is given a 20-minute bulk fermentation, then sheeted and chilled in a refrigerator or ice blankets for 30 minutes at 3 °C–4 °C. The dough is then processed using the **3-4-3** sequence resting in between every two folds in the freezer or ice blankets. When the pastry is made, it should again be rested for 30 minutes before sheeting in a freezer or ice blankets.

The pastry is then sheeted, cut, shaped, and placed in the proofer to 3/4 proof stage at a temperature of 26 °C –27 °C and relative humidity (RH) of 75% –80%. So, for example, if the normal proof time for your croissant is 120 minutes, for pre proofed, the time needs to be reduced to 90 minutes. The pastry should be egg washed and blast frozen for 30 minutes at a temperature of -18 °C –20 °C. Following the freezing process, the raw frozen croissants should be placed into a cardboard box with a plastic liner and sealed to prevent freezer burn. The frozen pre-proofed croissants should be stored at -18 °C until required. Frozen pre-proofed croissants should be removed from their cardboard storage box in the freezer. The pastries are then placed on baking trays and allowed to stand at room temperature for 10 minutes –15 minutes to defrost slightly. The croissants or other frozen pastry units can then be baked off at 170 °C –180 °C in a fan oven or 200 °C in a deck oven for approximately 20 minutes. Note that frozen/pre-proofed pastries with fillings, such as custard, jam, apple or other fruit fillings, may need a minimum of 30 minutes to defrost before baking.

Pre Proofed Frozen Croissant

Ingredients	1 Mix	1/2 Mix	Bakers % (Based on flour 100%)	Hydration %
	Kg / g	Kg / g	1000	50.00
Overnight dough Stage 1				
Strong flour	1,000	500	100.0 %	
Water	500	250	50.0 %	
Sugar	100	50	10.0 %	
Fresh yeast	50	25	5.0 %	
Fresh sourdough starter 50/50	200	100	20.0 %	
Improver	10	5	1.0 %	
Salt	18	9	1.8 %	
Milk powder	40	20	4.0 %	
Butter	50	25	5.0 %	
Dough head weight	1,968	984	Butter on Dough %	Total Butter % in both Dough & Lamination
Lamination dough Stage 2				
Laminating butter	500	250	25.4	30.4
Total batch weight	2,468	1,234		
Yield	33	16		
Scaling wt in grams	75			

18. Making Croissants and Viennoiserie Using Sourdough

It is possible to make croissant and viennoiserie using only natural sourdough, using dosage levels of up to 28% of total flour weight and eliminating yeast from the mix. The recipe below will produce excellent croissants when using the overnight fermentation method detailed earlier in the book. But this process will take three days as the pastry is made as follows using the **3-4-3** system.

Day1: Feed the starter, leave for 6 hours, then make the dough. Ferment for 2 –3 hours, chill overnight at 3 °C.

Day2: Make butter block, do a lock in-**3,** then laminate with a 4-fold, followed by a 3-fold. Rest in the refrigerator for 40 minutes. Shape and wrap in plastic 20 °C –22 °C for 5 –6 hours, then place in the refrigerator overnight at 3 °C (you may also use **5-4-3** or any other lamination system you want).

Day 3: Remove from refrigerator, egg wash and stand for 40 minutes to 1 hour. Proof until they jiggle. Please note that the final proof could take an additional 5 hours –7 hours, not a product for the faint-hearted due to the 3 days required to produce them. Bake the croissants in a fan oven at 175 °C –180 °C or a deck oven at 200 °C.

Notes on Sourdough Croissant Production

The high butter content in the recipe will inhibit/slow down drastically the fermentation of natural sourdough. The sourdough should be very active and refreshed at least twice for 3.5 hours between feeds and allowed to expand 2.5 –3 times its mixed size for 3 hours at a time before mixing it into the croissant dough. The target pH 4.1 of the sourdough should be at when adding to the croissant dough. The sourdough should not be too acidic as it will cause the dough to collapse during extended fermentation. The dough should be mixed in the manner specified earlier, without the addition of commercial yeast and allowed to ferment for 2 hours –3 hours at 20 °C –22 °C then overnight in a refrigerator at 3 °C –4 °C. The dough can then be processed as normal, but it may take up to three times longer to proof (between 5 hours –6 hours+). Check using the wobble test link page 87.

100% Sourdough Croissant

Ingredients	1 MIX Kg / g	1/2 Mix Kg / g	Bakers % (Based on flour 100%)	Hydration %
			1000	49.60
Overnight dough Stage 1				
Strong flour	1,000	500	100.0 %	
Milk	320	160	32.0 %	
Water	176	88	17.6 %	
Sugar	126	63	12.6 %	
Fresh sourdough starter 50/50	286	143	28.6 %	
Malt liquid	2	1	0.2 %	
Salt	16	8	1.6 %	
Butter	50	25	5.0 %	
Dough head weight	1,976	988	Butter on Dough %	Total Butter % in both Dough & Lamination
Lamination dough Stage 2				
Laminating butter	550	275	27.8	32.8
Total batch weight	2,526	1,263		
Yield	34	17		
Scaling wt in grams	75			

19. Sweet Puff Paste 3-4-4 / 4

First **3** lock-in   1st stage of the process –3 layers

Second 4-fold   3 × 4 layers = 12 layers -3 where dough touches dough = 9 layers

Third 4-fold   9 × 4 layers = 36 layers -3 where dough touches dough = 33 layers

Resting phase /.   Wrap in plastic, place in the refrigerator at 3 °C for 30 –40 minutes

Fourth 4-fold   33 × 4 layers = 132 layers -3 where dough touches dough = 129 layers.

Puff paste is not as time-consuming as it is made out to be and when made with butter. It is a delightful product that has many amazing possibilities. Using the folding numerical sequences detailed earlier, puff paste may be produced both swiftly and efficiently. The dough should ideally be mixed the day before and stored overnight in a refrigerator at 3 °C –4 °C. The dough is then removed from the refrigerator, and the butter block is placed over the dough's centre. The pastry is then folded into a **3 lock-in.** The dough is then sheeted, and a 4-fold is given to the dough. The dough is then given another 4 -fold, and at this stage, the block of pastry should be placed in the freezer wrapped in plastic for a half-hour or placed between two ice blankets for 20 minutes. The butter puff paste is now at the halfway stage.

After resting in the freezer, the pastry can be sheeted once more and given its final 4-fold. The pastry should then be placed in the freezer or between ice blankets for a further 45 minutes and can be processed or frozen. If the pastry is to be processed at this stage, the pastry should be allowed to rest for 1 hour before baking to prevent shrinkage or overnight in a refrigerator after sheeting and cutting.

Sweet Puff Paste Dough

Ingredients	1 Mix	1/2 Mix	Bakers % (Based on flour 100%)	Hydration %
	Kg / g	Kg / g	1000	53.00
Overnight dough Stage 1				
Strong flour	1,000	500	100.0 %	
Water	460	230	46.0 %	
Egg	70	35	7.0 %	
Sugar	20	10	2.0 %	
Butter unsalted	60	30	6.0 %	
Salt	20	10	2.0 %	
Dough head weight	1,630	815	**Butter on Dough %**	**Total Butter % in both Dough & Lamination**
Lamination dough Stage 2				
Laminating butter	1,000	500	61.3	67.3
Total batch weight	2,630	1,315		
Yield	35	18		
Scaling wt in grams	75			

Palmiers

Palmiers are made from a sweet puff pastry recipe. They are a personal favourite, which brings back childhood memories every time I eat them. When the puff pastry is made, copious quantities of sugar should be shaken over the  work surface and applied to the pastry following sheeting of the third 4-fold. The sugar should also be gently squeezed into the pastry at this stage using light pressure from a rolling pin or on a sheeter. The pastry should be folded one final time and sheeted once more to 4 mm thick covered, with copious quantities of sugar which should be rolled into the pastry. The pastry is allowed to rest for one more hour in a refrigerator before its final sheeting. Puff paste with the added sugar should be handled carefully and sheeted out to a thickness of 3.5 –4 cm. More sugar is applied over all the pastry and gently rolled into the pastry surfaces using a rolling pin before shaping into palmiers.

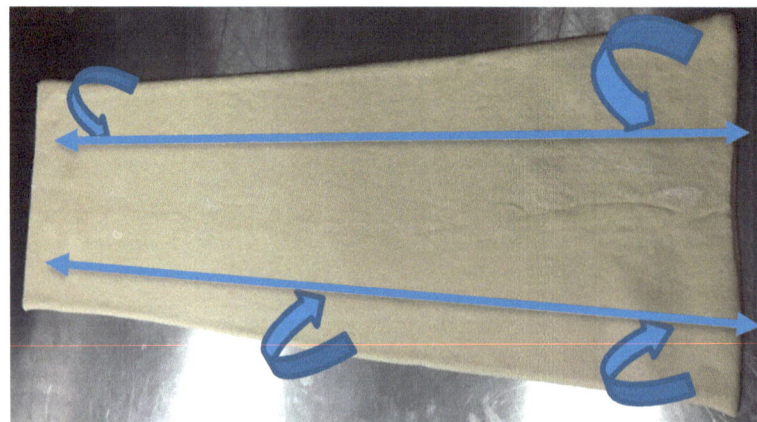

The pastry sheet is folded from the top of the rectangle and the bottom of the rectangle roughly one quarter into the pastry sheet. Both quarters are then folded into the sheet's centre, allowing some space for the final fold over. The top is again sprinkled with sugar, folded over once more to meet the pastry's bottom.

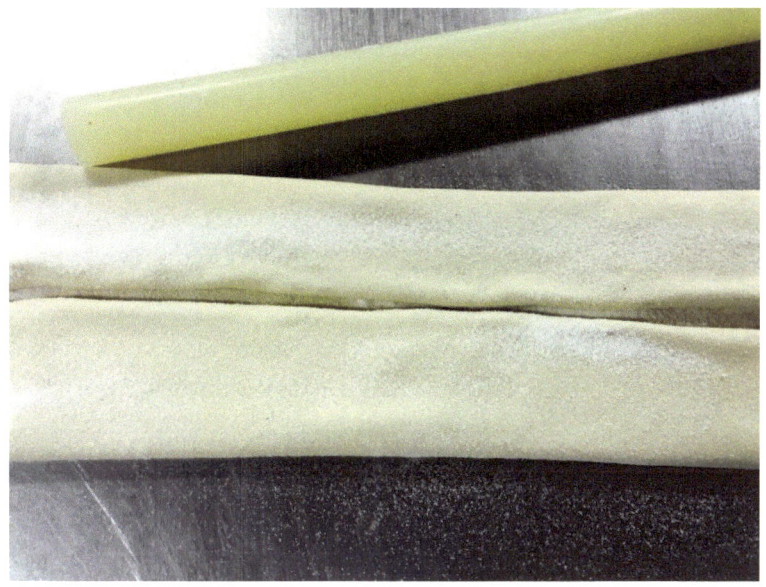

The cross-section of the pastry will have 6 layers or pleats of pastry for making the perfect palmier. The pastry should be wrapped tightly in parchment paper and chilled for half an hour before cutting. The palmiers should be cut into fingers 3 cm wide and placed cut edge facing upwards on trays allowing ample room for the pastry to expand during baking.

The palmiers are baked in a rack or deck oven at a temperature of 190 °C –200 °C for 20 minutes. Bake until a golden colour is achieved. Following baking, the pastry should be allowed to cool slightly on the tray and removed to a wire rack to prevent the pastry from becoming soggy. They can be sold individually, sandwiched with cream, or sealed into plastic bags to prevent them from absorbing moisture from the air. I have also added a video to my YouTube channel to follow how-to fold, form and cut the Butterfly Palmiers. Follow this link below.

https://www.youtube.com/watch?v=QqMIMygTaEM.

20. Savoury Puff Paste Recipe 3-4-4 / 4

I have included a savoury recipe for puff paste. This recipe makes good pastry for savoury products, including sausage rolls. I have included it as a cheaper option to the extra flaky pastry on page 113, which is a premium and expensive pastry due to the large quantities of butter and egg in the recipe. The hydration comparison is interesting when compared to the extra flaky puff paste. The larger quantity of butter in the extra flaky recipe lowers the hydration, making the pastry very crispy indeed.

Savoury Puff Paste

Ingredients	1 MIX	1/2 mix	Bakers %	Hydration %
	Kg / g	Kg / g	1000	60.30
Overnight dough Stage 1				
Bread flour	1,000	500	100.0 %	
Egg	455	228	45.5 %	
Water	148	74	14.8 %	
Butter unsalted	60	30	6.0 %	
Salt	20	10	2.0 %	
Dough head weight	1,683	842	Butter on Dough %	Total Butter % in both Dough & Lamination
Lamination dough Stage 2				
Laminating butter	1,000	500	59.4	65.4
Total batch weight	2,683	1,342		
Yield	36	18		
Scaling wt in grams	75			

21. Extra Flaky Puff Paste 3-3-3 / 3-3

I make a beautiful quiche filling with 250 g double cream, 250 g milk, 175 g egg, 10 g salt and 2g pepper. This base is rich and creamy, and both vegetarian and meat accompaniments are fantastic when used with this pastry recipe. It melts in your mouth, leaving you seeking another, as the rich flavour stays on your palate too long! Patience is key with this pastry. The dough is made on day one, the lamination, and the baking, the following day. The pastry is very flaky, a joy to eat. The filling for cheese and onion quiche is white onion 300 g red onion 300 g, butter 50 g, balsamic vinegar 50 g, salt 2.5 g, black pepper 1.5 g fry together and reduced in a frying pan. Allow the fillings to cool. Line a 32 cm quiche dish with puff paste. Add the cooled, fried onion mix. Pour the quiche base mix into the quiche dish, fill to 4/5ths. Sprinkle 60 g of grated Gruyere cheese on the top and bake for 45 minutes −50 minutes at 180 °C. You can also use broccoli/courgettes/mushrooms/tomato/bacon/ham or any other fillings you like in the quiche. Try both large and mini quiche and experiment with your favourite fillings. Equally, the pastry can be used to make delicious bases and even Portuguese custard tarts.

22. Puff Paste Quiche with Cheese and Onion

This recipe makes hands down the best puff pastry I have ever eaten. Light, crispy and really melt in the mouth, this pastry is perfect for those luxury puff pastry goodies you want to make. It is versatile and can be used for both sweet and savoury goods. Try Vol au Vents with chicken and mushroom, sausage rolls to die for and of course, the quiche featured here or with other fillings of your choice. It will not disappoint. Recently. I made Christmas mince pies with this recipe, and it did not disappoint.

Extra Flaky Puff Paste

Ingredients	1 Mix	1/2 Mix	Bakers % (Based on flour 100%)	Hydration %
	Kg / g	Kg / g	1000	35.30
Overnight dough Stage 1				
Soft biscuit flour	1,000	500	100.0 %	
Egg	205	103	20.5 %	
Water	148	74	14.8 %	
Sugar	68	34	6.8 %	
Butter unsalted	375	188	37.5 %	
Salt	14	7	1.4 %	
Dough head weight	1,810	905	**Butter on Dough %**	**Total Butter % in both Dough & Lamination**
Lamination dough Stage 2				
Laminating butter	500	250	27.6	65.1
Total batch weight	2,310	1,155		
Yield	31	15		
Scaling wt in grams	75			

Mix all ingredients in a bowl, except the unsalted butter. Ensure that the butter is at room temperature. Using the hook attachment, mix Stage 1 on a dough mixer for 4 minutes on slow speed and 3 minutes on 2nd speed, adding the butter when the dough comes together. Mix to clear. Pinout the dough to 12 mm, cover with plastic and store in the refrigerator covered for at least 30 minutes or overnight. Prepare the butter block in a rectangular shape and store it in the refrigerator until the dough is ready to laminate. Begin with a 3 lock-in. The Lamination sequences are split into two resting stages indicated after the third 3-fold in the sequence by a separator or /.

The rolling sequence for this type of puff paste is a **3**-3-3 / 3-3- sequence.

First 3-fold the lock-in - **3** layers

Second 3-fold 3 x 3 layers = 9 layers – 2 points where dough touches dough = 7 layers

Third 3-fold 7 x 3 layers = 21 layers – 2 points where dough touches dough = 19 layers

It is important to rest the dough for at least half an hour in a refrigerator before giving it the remaining two folds.

Fourth 3-fold 19 × 3 layers = 57 layers–2 points where dough touches dough= 55 layers.

Fifth 3-fold 55 × 3 layers = 165 layers–2 points where dough touches dough=163 layers.

Chill in the refrigerator for 45 –60 minutes and sheet to make quiche, sausage roll and a range of assorted goods.

The 3-4-4 / 4 system

The dough should ideally be mixed the day before and stored overnight in a refrigerator at 3 °C –4 °C. The dough is then removed from the refrigerator, and the butter block placed over the centre of the dough and folded into a **3** for the lock-in. The pastry is then sheeted to 4 mm, and a further 4-fold is given to the pastry. The pastry is then sheeted once more and given another 4-fold, and at this stage, the pastry block should be placed in the freezer wrapped in plastic for a half-hour or placed between two ice blankets for 20 minutes. The butter puff paste requires one last fold to complete the lamination sequence. After resting in the freezer, the block of dough can be given a final 4-fold. The dough should then be placed in the freezer or between ice blankets for a further 40 minutes and can be processed or frozen. If the pastry is to be processed at this stage, the pastry should be sheeted, cut and rested for 1 hour before baking to prevent pastry shrinkage. The cut units can also be left overnight in a refrigerator and baked off the following day.

23. Laminated Brioche

Laminated brioche is a very highly enriched pastry made with a butter brioche dough plus 50.7% butter based on total dough weight. The pre-dough starter contains water, but the main dough liquids include milk, eggs, and egg yolks. The higher hydration laminated brioche pastries are popular throughout France and Europe and command a great price for the quality of ingredients and the process used. Laminated brioche can also be used to make the legendary "Cronut ™" style product, where the pastry is proofed and then float fried instead of baked. Laminated brioche can be sold in small or larger units, typically baked in a fluted brioche shape of which there are an infinite amount of sizes. Individual brioche is made similarly to pain aux raisins, rolled into a sheet, then coiled up and cut into pieces. The smaller ones are 2 cm wide and weighed 60 g, the larger ones are 600 g, and the shape I used was 25 cm wide at the top. Brioche shapes can be purchased in metal, and there are also one-use disposable cardboard ones coated with silicone. I used these disposable ones in the photos on page 115 –116.

Laminated Brioche

Ingredients	1 Mix	1/2 Mix	Bakers % (Based on flour 100%)	Hydration %
	Kg / g	Kg / g	1420	65.63
Predough Stage 1				
Bakers flour	160	80	11.3 %	
Water	100	50	7.0 %	
Fresh yeast	3	2	0.2 %	
Salt	3	2	0.2 %	
	266	133		
Dough Stage 2				
Predough	266	133	18.7	
Strong flour	1,260	630	88.7 %	
Milk	192	96	13.5 %	
Egg yolk	80	40	5.6 %	
Whole egg	560	280	39.4 %	
Sugar	180	90	12.7 %	
Fresh yeast	63	32	4.4 %	
Malt liquid	25	13	1.8 %	
Salt	27	14	1.9 %	
Butter	227	114	16.0 %	
Dough head weight	2,880	1,440	Butter on Dough %	Total Butter % in both Dough & Lamination
Lamination dough Stage 3				
Laminating butter	1,000	500	34.7	50.7
Total batch weight	3,880	1,940		
Yield brioche 60g	65	32		
Scaling wt in grams	60			
Yield brioche 600g	6	3		
Scaling wt in grams	600			

The laminated brioche dough should be kept chilled at all stages of the lamination process, as outlined earlier in this book, by keeping the enriched dough. The lamination sequence for the small pieces is **3**-4-3 or **5-4-3** for larger pieces. Laminated brioche is typically sold plain, without filling, and due to the high levels of enrichment, will keep well if packaged in a re-sealable plastic bag.

24. Kouign Amann 3-4-4

Raspberry rhubarb Kouign amann in the photo to the left. The Kouign amann was invented in 1860, a speciality pastry of the town of Douarnenez in Finistère, Brittany, France (Lonely Planet Food, 2017). This delicious creation is credited to Baker Yves-René Scordia (1828 –1878). The name originates from the Breton language combining the words for cake (kouign) and butter (amann). Kouign-amann is a round crusty pastry, originally made from bread dough but made today using a rich viennoiserie dough. The Kouign-amann is a form of laminated brioche with many butter and sugar layers folded in, similar manner to puff pastry, although with less laminated layers. Salted butter is used in the pastry and greases the 7 cm wide × 4 cm high metal rings used to bake the Kouign-amann.

The pastry is a three-day process. Day 1, the pre-dough is made and fermented at 19 °C overnight. Day 2, the dough is mixed in two stages, 4 minutes on slow, 5 minutes on 2nd speed, ensuring that the dough is well developed before adding the butter and mixing to clear for a further 3minutes –4 minutes. The DDT is 26 °C, and the dough should be fermented in bulk for 45 minutes at room temperature, then placed in the refrigerator at 3 °C overnight. The pastry is made using the **3-4-4** laminating system, but copious amounts of sugar are added to the sheeted pastry before the final 4-fold. The pastry is sheeted to 4 mm, cut into 10 cm squares, roughly 75 g each. The four corners are then folded to the centre, and the pastry is placed in the steel rings. The pastry is proofed at a low temperature of 25 °C –26

°C and low humidity 60% –65% to ensure that the salted butter layers and the sugar do not melt before baking. Toppings applied before baking included crème pâtissière, apple, Nutella, raspberry/rhubarb and chopped raspberry pear marinade on page 126. They are slowly baked at 190 °C for 20 –25 minutes until the pastry achieves maximum oven spring and the sugar caramelises. The baked pastry resembles a laminated muffin-shape and is essentially a salted caramelised croissant in a round shape. Kerrygold Irish butter was used in this recipe, but any salted high-fat butter will work well.

The buttered-sugared shapes for Kouign amann left; above a selection of different flavours and a proofed pastry in its buttered/sugared ring. Use coarse sugar if available.

Kougin-Amann			Based on flour 100%	
Ingredients	1 Mix	1/2 Mix	Bakers %	Hydration %
	Kg / g	Kg / g	700	54.57
Predough Stage 1				
Bakers flour	70	35	10.0 %	
Water	46	23	6.6 %	
Fresh yeast	1.2	0.6	0.2 %	
Salt	2	1.0	0.3 %	
	119	60		
Dough Stage 2				
Predough	119	60	17.0	
Strong flour	630	315	90.0 %	
Milk	96	48	13.7 %	
Egg yolk	40	20	5.7 %	
Whole egg	200	100	28.6 %	
Sugar	90	45	12.9 %	
Fresh yeast	32	16	4.6 %	
Malt liquid	13	7	1.9 %	
Salt	12	6	1.7 %	
Butter Addition Stage 3				
Butter	114	57	16.3 %	
Dough Head Weight	1,346	673	Butter on Dough %	Total Butter % in Both Dough & Lamination
Lamination Stage 4				
Kerrygold Salted Butter	500	250	37.1	53.4
Total Batch Weight	1,846	923		
Yield 75 g	25	12		
Scaling wt in grams	75			

Coupe du Monde Chocolatine, Toulouse, France. 2019

An invitation came from Toulouse, France, to participate in the Coupe du Monde Chocolatine (CDMC) or the World Cup Chocolatine Championships from the organiser, Geraldine Laborde. I accepted the invitation and the competition challenge and used the invitation as a great reason to motivate me into top-level competition mode once more. I had not competed in over 25 years, but I decided to rise to the challenge and practised daily from April until the end of May. I travelled to Toulouse and enjoyed the company of Geraldine and her little dog Marvel. She brought me to the old city where she went to the hairdressers, and I went off with her dog Marvel to do some sightseeing. Toulouse is a beautiful old city with a massive square which houses the Townhall and many architecturally historic and important buildings. There is much to see and do in Toulouse, beautiful open-air spaces where one can dine alfresco, and people watch as well as century-old churches and a great choice of shops. We met up with Geraldine's friends and later went for a meal and to a Scottish bar for a drink.

Geraldine took me to the centre of Toulouse, where the yellow jacket protesters were in full swing. Robo-cop type police wearing full riot gear in the hundreds were also present, and the vans which had transported them to the city were parked as far as the eye could see. It was a surreal experience. I kept away from all the battles which were breaking out between police and protesters and took refuge with Geraldine on the first floor of an Irish Pub as water cannons and tear gas were used by the police. I witnessed many baton charges and could smell the sickly tear gas as it permeated the building. Outside was a warzone, and I wondered how long it would take to be safe to leave. Two hours later, after a light lunch, the crowds had dispersed, and we walked through the city. All the banks and multinational companies such as Burger King, McDonald's and many others were closed and boarded up with wooden shutters. It was sad to see this, but the French have even back to revolution days been very vociferous about political matters and are prepared to fight for what they think is right. The following morning, I went back to a local baker called David, who opened his production facility to some competitors. We prepared our doughs and ingredients for the world championship the day before the competition. At David's bakery, I met with fellow competitor Christophe Secondi from Corsica, and we hit it off as buddies straight away. Christophe would travel to Galway later in the year to visit me with his family. Having completed preparations for the event, all candidates were invited on a walking tour of Toulouse, and we even got to sample a special local delicacy of chocolatine ice cream. We all had dinner al fresco in a square off the main thoroughfare and got to chat and meet with members of the jury and other competitors. I returned early to the hotel to get a good night's sleep and prepare for the competition, the world championships beckoned, and I wanted to be on top of my game on the day.

The Coupe du Monde Chocolatine was a true artisan competition. It tested one's manual skills and abilities to the limit. Apart from mixing and ingredient preparation, all lamination, butter preparation, cutting and shaping had to be done by hand with a rolling pin, and mechanical lamination machines were not allowed. Very stringent rules regarding the quantity of dough and the baked weight of the pieces were strictly enforced. Each candidate was assigned a supervisor to ensure that all work followed the rules and very high hygiene and professionalism level. Over 40 bakers from several nations competed on the day in two shifts as there was limited equipment and space for all to work simultaneously. I had rehearsed my pastries' production many times and launched into my four allocated hours of production time.

I finished with 10 minutes to spare and was very pleased with my results. I would miss the tasting and marking by the 48-jury member panel and the prize-giving ceremony as I had to fly to the UK for some classes. I left for the airport in Toulouse and took my first leg flight, which touched down at Brussels airport and decided to get a bite to eat. As I was eating my pasta in the restaurant, my phone rang, and it was Geraldine Laborde who called to inform me of my silver medal placing in the world championships. I was over the moon with excitement and did not expect a podium finish. I was absolutely delighted with my result and felt joy, privilege, and success had come my way. Now I will share my recipe with you, which won me the *"World Silver Medal, Coupe Du Monde Chocolatine 2019"*.

25. World Silver Medal 2019 Coupe du Monde Chocolatine 3-4-4

The chocolatine classique is a masterpiece of French ingenuity and creativity. Also known as pain au chocolat globally and in France, this viennoiseries' identity is on a par with the croissant worldwide as another iconic French classic. It is enjoyed not only as a breakfast pastry globally but also as a sweet treat by millions of people at any time of the day. My  recipe makes two dough heads at 700 g each, add 200 g butter for each dough head for the lamination. This recipe gives 2 × 12 pieces. I use the same base recipe for both doughs.

Ingredients for Chocolatine	Quantity grams	%	Production method 3-4-4 Lamination system
Gruau flour T-45	365	45,6	Mix for 8 minutes 1st speed, 5 minutes 2nd speed
Tradition flour T-55	365	45,6	on a planetary mixer with a dough hook.
Water	300	37,5	Desired dough temperature is 24°C.
Liquid levain	140	17,5	Scale 1 x 700g head of dough.
Sugar	104	13	Place in a container overnight, covered with plactic.
Yeast (fresh)	32	4	Leave in refrigerator @2°C overnight. Laminate 3-4-4, cool
Malt (liquid)	2	0,3	down again for 45 minutes 2°C. Sheet out to 12mm
Salt	14	1,8	after 25 minutes. Roll to 3mm, cut 14cm long x 8cm wide
Butter	80	10	Using 2 bars of chocolate provided (6g each), shape the
Pat fermentée	4	0,5	chocolatines. Each unbaked chocolatine should weigh between
Use 700 g dough to 200 g butter			68-71g. Final proof 2-2.5 hours @ 27°C. Egg wash, rest for 10
Lamination butter % dough weight	2 x 200	28,4	minutes. Bake in convection oven 17-18 minutes @ 170°C

Physical and Flavour Characteristics

An external aspect includes the light crispy crumb combined with the natural brilliance of the egg wash on the hand-laminated butter pastry. The addition of malt to the dough accelerates the Maillard reaction during baking, giving a pleasing chestnut colour to the exterior crust and enhancing flavour. Finally, a layer of chocolate croissant dough highlights the flavour, colour, lamination and exquisite internal honeycomb texture. The baked chocolatine is allowed to cool and is then carefully stencilled using a small sprinkle of icing sugar with a 4-leaf clover design (page 121) for greater eye appeal.

Description

The Orange chocolate praline twist is a variation of the original, but out of respect to the original, all of the elements of making this classic are retained, while other features are added. A thin sheet of chocolate dough is placed on the laminated dough just before sheeting, and when cut into rectangles, the dough then is cut into five even pieces. The middle three are twisted twice, giving this innovative chocolatine a special twist. Extra crispiness and texture are added from cocoa's light dust, icing sugar and orange bubble sugar after baking. This recipe makes 2 dough heads at 700 g add 200 g butter for each dough head's lamination. This recipe gives 2 × 12 pieces. I use the same base recipe for both doughs. Special instructions for the chocolate dough are on the next page.

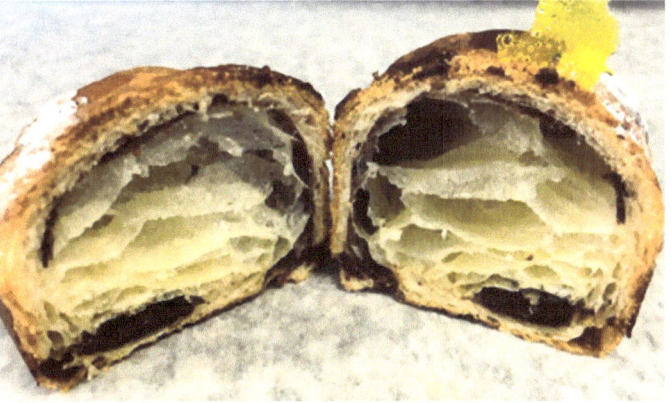

Ingredients for innovative Chocolatine	Quantity grams	%	Production method 3-4-4 lamination system
Gruau flour T-45	365	45.6	Mix for 8 minutes 1st speed, 5 minutes 2nd speed using a
Tradition flour T-55	365	45.6	planetary mixer with a dough hook
Water	300	37.5	Desired dough temperature is 24°C
Liquid levain	140	17.5	Scale 1 x 700 g head of dough, make 155 g chocolate
Sugar	104	13	dough. Place in a container covered with plastic
Yeast (fresh)	32	4	Leave in the refrigerator @2-3°C overnight. Laminate 3-4-4,
Malt (liquid)	2	0.3	cool down again for 45 minutes @2-3°C. Sheet out to 12mm
Salt	14	1.8	after 25 minutes. Roll to 3mm, cut 14cm long x 8cm wide
Butter	80	10	Cut into 5 strands, twist the middle 3, roll up using 1-12 g bar
Pat fermentée	4	0.5	of chocolate. Each chocolatine should weigh between 78-88 g
Use 700 g dough to 200 g butter			Final proof 2-2.5 hours @ 27°C. Egg wash, rest for 10 minutes
Chocolate Dough Method:			After mixing for 8 minutes, remove 120 g of the croissant dough
Dough from the mix above	120		from the mix to make the chocolate dough
Cocoa Powder	10		Add the rest of the ingredients to the 120 g of dough
Butter	10		Continue to mix for 5 minutes on slow speed
Water	5		Mix to clear, This is the chocolate dough for the bicolor
Fresh Yeast	10		Bulk ferment with the white dough and chill overnight

Physical and Flavour Characteristics

Moulds were specially created to enable this chocolatine to keep its shape. External aspects include the three twists of this bicolour dough in the centre and the careful dusting after baking of dark Dutch cocoa, icing sugar, homemade candied orange and bubble sugar, which mirrors the light internal texture. Finally, a layer of chocolate croissant dough highlights the flavour, colour and lamination aspect of the internal texture.

The Added Value of The Product

The innovative chocolatine can cool and is then carefully stencilled, with icing sugar on one side and cocoa. Candied peel is added to the centre, and a touch of orange bubble sugar gives this chocolate a unique finish and beautiful textures in the palm on the pallet.

Description

After 8 minutes of mixing the dough recipe on 1st speed, I remove a piece of dough from the mix, weighing 120 g. I prepare 12 g cocoa powder, 10 g butter, 5 g of water and 10 g fresh yeast, and when the main dough is mixed, I put the 120 g of dough into the bowl with the cocoa mix and mix together for 5 minutes on 2nd speed to get a nice chocolate dough mix which I will use to top the pastry once it is laminated. I carefully scale the white dough with the chocolate dough to ensure I have just the 700 g required for the competition. The small remaining piece, 37 g of white dough, is kept as a pâté fermentée for use in the next dough, so there is no wastage.

Shaping The Innovative Chocolatine

The chocolatine pastry is rolled to 3.5 mm with the chocolate side down and then cut into 12 pieces of approximately 14 cm × 8 cm; each is then divided into five. The central three strands are twisted three times. The homemade chocolate bar is added. The chocolatine is then rolled up and placed in a special metal form to prevent the sides from falling over and retain the chocolate shape/aspect.

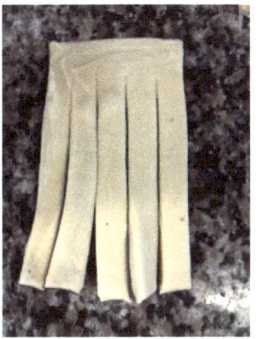 

Recipe for handmade 12 g chocolate bars	Quantity g	Production method chocolate bars
Chocolate noir	120	Break up the chocolate and melt to 45°C. Do not exceed this temperature
Praline hazelnut paste	40	Add the orange oil
Roasted nibbed hazelnut	100	Add the praline
Orange oil	2	Blend the crushed, roasted, nibbed hazelnuts
Yield 21 bars @ 12 g each		Pipe into 12 g bars in silicone moulds, cool in the freezer
Bubble sugar recipe	**g**	**Production method bubble sugar**
	100	Blitz the isomalt and the orange colour in a blender
Isomalt	1	Add a drop of orange oil. Place a teaspoon of the mixture into macaron silicone
Orange powder colour	1	mat indents 2cm wide. Melt in the oven @185°C for 7-10 minutes, add a whole,
Orange oil		roasted hazelnut when melted. Allow to cool slightly, and remove from the
Yield 30 discs		silicone shape. Add to the chocolatine adding a strip of candied orange to finish.

The Special Shape for the "Innovative Chocolatine" Challenge

Especially for this competition, I got 12 × 2 mm thick stainless-steel shapes made. The moulds are 80 mm wide, 80 mm long, and 75 mm deep on the outside. Proofing and baking in these moulds prevent the ends from falling over and distorting the shape. The result is a distinctly similar shape to the original chocolatine, but with a twist. I wanted to create a new chocolatine that keeps all the aspects of the chocolatine we all know and love but set this one apart as an innovative luxury version of the original classic, with a homemade crunchy praline orange bar. Colour, aspect, appearance and texture were given a lot of thought to reflect the flavours of orange, chocolate and hazelnut in this innovative chocolatine creation.

While innovative by nature, this chocolatine's shape and textures are true to the original creation of what one expects a chocolatine to be. The curved shape rolled about a chocolate bar, proofed and baked to perfection. The orange bubble sugar, roast hazelnut and candied orange strip reflected the flavours and honeycomb internal structure expected of a world-class chocolatine.

The Praline-Orange Chocolatine.

26. Raspberry Pear Marinade 3-4-3

The raspberry pear marinade has become one of my most recognisable pastries and a signature dish. The marinade is best made a few days before using the pears as the colour and flavours increase with age.

You will need two small tins of pear halves. There are usually 6 pear halves per small tin. You will also need 60 g sugar, 50 g frozen raspberries, 5 g raspberry alcohol and some vanilla to taste. The mixture is boiled and simmered for 5 minutes. The marinade for 12 pastries is made by the following method: The juice from the tinned pears is strained into a saucepan. The sugar and raspberry purée is added to the pear juice, the vanilla is then added, and the mixture is brought to the boil and allowed to simmer for 5 minutes. The syrup should be set aside to cool, at which point the Raspberry alcohol is added, and finally the pears. The pink syrup mixture with the pears should be placed in a sealed container, covered and put in the refrigerator at 3 °C for 2 days to ensure the pears' correct colouration. You will need to make crème pâtissière to pipe and freeze as 5 cm mini eclairs in advance. I have made a YouTube video on how to pipe the frozen crème pâtissière bars, see link for making frozen créme pâtissière pieces for viennoiserie https://youtu.be/kwUZEcjtak4 on my YouTube channel.

27. The Crème Pâtissière Recipe 414 g

Stage1: Mix together to form a paste

125 g	Milk	Whisk and boil together; prepare stage 2
25 g	Sugar	

Stage 2: Whisk all stage 2 together and add to stage 1

25 g	Caster sugar
33 g	Flour soft wheat
50 g	Egg yolks (2 approx.)
125 g	Milk

Vanilla pod scraped (1g) to extract the seeds or use vanilla essence

Stage 3: Remove stages 1&2 from the heat and add the butter, whisk to clear.

30 g   Butter

Method Detail

Heat the stage 1 milk and half of the sugar to boiling point in a small saucepan. Weigh the rest of the stage 2 ingredients separately and whisk with a hand whisk to a fluffy and smooth mixture. Once the stage 1 milk/sugar boils, remove from the heat and pour the mixture from stage 2 into the saucepan and whisk gently. Put the pan on the heat again and keep stirring with the hand whisk until the mix thickens (generally, the cooking time is 2 –3 minutes per kilo of milk). Once cooked, take it off the heat and add the butter to it. Keep stirring until it is fully absorbed, spread the crème pâtissière onto a clean tray lined with clingfilm, and then dust with icing sugar to prevent skin from forming. Cover and place the crème pâtissière in the refrigerator to cool. When cool, store in a refrigerator then to use, beat the crème pâtissière on a stand mixer with a cake beater to soften it to piping consistency and pipe it into fingers as previously described and freeze.

Preparation and Cutting of The Pastry

For the raspberry pear viennoiserie, the pastry is sheeted to a thickness of 7 mm and chilled again for 20 minutes to stiffen the butter and the pastry dough to enable cutting without shrinking the pastry. Using a large pear-shaped or teardrop-shaped cutter 16 cm long × 10 cm wide, cut the bases and place them on a tray. The pear-shaped pastry pieces are placed on a tray with silicone paper, egg-washed and proofed at a temperature of 27 °C for 60 –90 minutes at 75% –80% relative humidity. The temperature is critical as, if it exceeds 28 °C, the butter will liquefy and run out of the dough, destroying the lamination layers.

When proofed, the frozen custard fingers are placed in the proofed pastry centre and given a gentle shove downwards to embed them into the pastry. The frozen custard fingers' function is to prevent the custard from leaking out over the edges as the pastry rises. Check out my YouTube channel below to see how the technique is done.

How to insert frozen crème pâtissière into proofed pastry https://youtu.be/NBm1Ti-YAWU

Raspberry Jam is then piped onto the frozen custard, and, finally, the rinsed, dried raspberry pears are sliced five times from right to left but leaving the upper part of the pear attached. The sliced raspberry pear is placed on the custard and pressed down to prevent it from falling over in the oven while baking.

Using a ventilated or fan oven, pre-set the temperature at 230 °C, load the pastry and close the oven door. Reset the temperature to 175 °C and bake for 22 minutes –24 minutes. The baked pastry should be allowed to cool, then glazed with nappage or apricot jam. Using a bench scraper, with the blade placed 3 mm from each pastry's edge at a 45° angle, the pastries are dusted with icing sugar. The same is done at the slender tip side of each pastry using a dusting of raspberry powder. Finally, a fresh raspberry is placed at the top of the baked pear on the pastry. If required, red chocolate hearts may also be sprinkled on the baked pear to finalise the garnish.

28. Chocolate Pear Baskets 3-4-3

It can also be made with chocolate…This creation is a delicate chocolate pear basket using the same teardrop-shaped cutter as above for the raspberry pear marinade. The thin end of the tear is rolled out thinly. Frozen crème pâtissière is placed on the pastry centre, followed by two small chocolate bars (1 Pain au Chocolat baton split in half) and a small pear half to cover both. The tip is stretched over the pear and tucked in under the pastry at the front, gently. As the pastry proofs, the tip gently releases from under the proofing pastry, and a handle appears to form on this beautifully tasty pastry.

To make a pear with raspberry jam variety, simply insert a disc of frozen crème pâtissière into the teardrop-shaped piece of pastry, add a half of a poached/tin pear, proof and bake. Add some raspberry jam on the inside, and after baking, a sprinkle of raspberry powder to garnish.

29. Pain Aux Raisins 3-4-3

Using the pastry recipe page 134, a 1/2 mix will make approximately 16 –18 units. Use the crème pâtissière recipe on page 127. Golden raisins are wonderful in this product and should be washed the day before use. Additionally, they can be soaked with a little rum for added flavour. Weigh all your ingredients and place them into the mixing bowl (except the lamination butter). Shape your butter into a rectangle butter block and place it in the refrigerator. Using the dough hook with an electric mixer, mix on slow speed for about 4 minutes or until the dough combines, then mix on 2nd speed until smooth (roughly 4 minutes). Roll the dough into a rectangular shape, place it into a plastic bag on a baking tray then place it in the refrigerator overnight. Remove the croissant dough out of the refrigerator, roll it out in a rectangle until it is twice the butter block's size. Make a Lock-in **3**. Slice the closed dough edges (sandwich method) to release the elastic recoil. Rotate the dough 90°, then sheet to 4 mm and make a 4-fold (approximately four times longer than when you first placed the butter in). Place the pastry back in the refrigerator to rest until it is cold (20 minutes–30 minutes). Cut the closed edges to ease the elastic recoil and sheet to 5 mm; make a 3-fold, rest in the refrigerator for up to 60 minutes at 3 °C.

For the sheeting stage, sheet the pastry to between 5 mm –6 mm thick to a rectangle (45 cm width). Spread crème pâtissière evenly, leaving a good 2 cm strip of the pastry free from crème pâtissière at the base, sprinkle raisins all over then start rolling firmly like a swiss roll, but not too tight from top to base. Roll towards yourself. It is easier! Mark and cut the roll into slices (2 cm –3 cm thick) using a very sharp serrated tooth knife. Tuck the ends to prevent them from opening up in the proof stage, then place them on baking trays using baking paper and place them in the proofer. Proof time can vary and can take up to 2.5 hours at 26 °C with 75% relative humidity. Remove the trays from the proofer, egg wash gently all over. Place trays in a pre-heated oven (210 °C for a deck oven, 180 °C for a fan oven) until you get a lovely golden-brown crust. Bake for approximately 15 minutes, depending on product size, to a golden-brown colour. When cool, brush with boiled apricot jam to finish; then drizzle with warm fondant or water icing, you can also garnish with a half glacé cherry.

Pain Aux Raisins

Ingredients	1 Mix	1/2 Mix	Based on flour 100%	
			Bakers %	Hydration %
	Kg / g	Kg / g	1000	48.50
Overnight dough Stage 1				
Strong flour	1,000	500	100.0 %	
Water	485	243	48.5 %	
Sugar	120	60	12.0 %	
Fresh yeast	40	20	4.0 %	
Salt	18	9	1.8 %	
Milk powder	30	15	3.0 %	
Dough head weight	1,693	847	**Butter on Dough %**	Total butter % in both Dough & Lamination
Lamination dough Stage 2				
Laminating butter	550	275	32.5	32.5
Total batch weight	2,243	1,122		
Yield	32	16		
Scaling wt in grams	70			
Additions to the pastry:				
Crème pâtissière	1000g	500g		
Raisins	600g	300g		

30. Cinnamon Swirls 3-4-3

Cinnamon swirls are a delicious alternative for those who do not like raisins or other dried fruits. They are made up exactly the same way as pain aux raisins. Use the 1/2 recipe on page 136 for the pastry. The crème pâtissière (page 127) is mixed with cinnamon sugar (page 136) to make the cinnamon custard. The cinnamon custard is spread on the pastry, allowing a good 2 cm of the pastry free of cinnamon custard at the base, so it can be sealed. Moisten this piece of the pastry by brushing with a damp pastry brush; then, start rolling the pastry towards you like a Swiss roll (not too tight) from top to base. Cut the roll into slices (2 cm -3 cm thick), tucking the tails under the pastry's main body to prevent them from opening during proof. Then place them on baking trays using baking paper and place them in the proofer. Proof and bake the same as the pain aux raisins in the previous recipe. For extra crunchiness, nibbed or crushed sugar can be added just before baking. This way, the sugar remains crispy and crunchy and doesn't dissolve as it would if left standing for some time before baking. The Cinnamon sugar recipe is at the bottom of the Cinnamon Swirls recipe.

Cinnamon Swirls

Ingredients	1 Mix	1/2 Mix	Bakers % (Based on flour 100%)	Hydration %
	Kg / g	Kg / g	1000	48.50
Overnight dough Stage 1				
Strong flour	1,000	500	100.0 %	
Water	485	243	48.5 %	
Sugar	120	60	12.0 %	
Fresh yeast	40	20	4.0 %	
Salt	18	9	1.8 %	
Milk powder	30	15	3.0 %	
Dough head weight	1,693	847	**Butter on Dough %**	Total Butter % in both Dough & Lamination
Lamination dough Stage 2				
Laminating butter	550	275	32.5	32.5
Total batch weight	2,243	1,122		
Yield	32	16		
Scaling wt in grams	70			
Additions to the pastry:				
Cinnamon	40	20		
Brown sugar	160	80		
Crème pâtissière	1000	500		

Beautiful cinnamon custard is at the heart of these delicious cinnamon swirls. They are sprinkled on the top with crushed sugar just before baking. Otherwise, the sugar will dissolve on the egg wash and turn to syrup, which will run to the bottom of the pastry and burn it as it bakes.

Other Ideas to Stimulate the Mind

31. Apple Pistachio/Apple Raspberry

Apple-pistachio with crème pâtissière 3-4-3. These lovely pastries are cut from pastry sheeted to 5 mm thick using a Matfer brand oval-shaped-cutter. The oval cutter measurements I use are 12.5 cm long × 9 cm wide. The pastries are proofed without any toppings to full volume. Flat cut pastries like this take  less time to proof as there is only one layer of pastry, which is not coiled like a croissant and as a result, the core temperature rises quickly. They generally take 60 minutes −90 minutes to proof. Once proofed, they should be egg washed, and frozen crème pâtissière (page 127) bars should be placed inverted (top of frozen crème pâtissière) on the proofed dough and pressed into the pastry, so the flat base of the frozen custard is facing up. This flat surface is perfect for placing your sliced apples on. Use small apples when preparing the pastries, and I use half an apple sliced thinly on each pastry. Fan the apples out evenly and press fully down. The apple slices will stick to the egg wash and remain in place for the bake. Bake for 25 minutes at 180 °C −195 °C. The apple topping takes longer to bake than a plain croissant. Once baked and cooled, the pastries are glazed with apricot nappage and garnished with freshly ground pistachio nut to finish. A raspberry variety can also be made by adding raspberry jam under the apple before baking and dusting one side with raspberry powder. The other side is  dusted with icing sugar after baking, cooling and glazing with apricot jam.

32. Cappuccino Chocolatine - Three Types of Pastry

The Cappuccino Cream Chocolatine is made with three types of pastry combined, cappuccino coffee, chocolate and vanilla pastry. Each pastry has three types of butter, chocolate butter, instant coffee butter and plain butter. Add vanilla to the dough for extra flavour. Lamination sequence for each dough is **3**-4 (9 layers) stack on top of each other (3 × 9 = 27)-2 DTP, total layers 25, same as croissant **3**-4-3. Sheet out, cut, proof and bake. Finish as above, or use your imagination for a personalised finish.

33. Raspberry/Strawberry Chocolatine

Made using 10% raspberry or strawberry powder in the butter. The pastry is then laminated 3-4-4 to produce 33 fruit flavoured strawberry layers. This chocolatine also has raspberry jam as a filling and was made using my croissant recipe on page 52. Cut, shape, proof and bake as per chocolatine.

34. Strawberry Shortcake

Vanilla streusel recipe- use pastry flour
Stage 1
Butter 100 g — Cream the butter and sugar together
Sugar 100 g
Vanilla 2 g — or use vanilla essence
Stage 2
Flour 125 g — Add to above and mix to a paste
Freeze until required. Alternatively mix to a crumb and refrigerate until required
Triangle steel shapes 10 cm length × 4.5 cm high

This triangle-shaped viennoiserie has a laminated pastry base, chocolate brioche middle layer, strawberry puree/jam and topped with vanilla streusel, then sprinkled with icing sugar and pistachio post bake. The base was cut out of croissant dough 4 mm thick; the brioche was cut out 3 mm thick, and the strawberry puree piped on the brioche. Proof for 90 minutes at 26 °C –27 °C. The streusel is applied just before baking. Bake at 200 °C –20 minutes.

35. Nutella/Coffee

Made using an infused butter; 10% instant coffee in the lamination butter and the pastry recipe on page 52, this praline style chocolatine had Nutella piped inside after baking and cooling. A swirl of buttercream, chocolate flake and hazelnut to decorate. The pastry is then dusted with cocoa powder and a light over dust of sweet white icing sugar. The combination of all the flavours makes this pastry a marvellous accompaniment with your favourite flavoured coffee. It can also be made in a twin laminated variety, with plain pastry and coffee infused butter forming two halves of the one pastry. Both are laminated separately using the 3-3-3 system.

Both the coffee pastry and the plain pastry have 19 layers and when both are fused/assembled together, you end up with 37 layers (we take away one dough touching point) when we stack the two types of pastry on top of each other. Cut 8 cm wide and 12cm-16 cm long, depending on how big you want them to be.

36. Raspberry Brioche Sablée

Possibly one of my favourite viennoiseries and taught to me by my dear friend François Wolfisberg, who is located in Carouge, Switzerland. François and I met in the late 1990s as fellow competitors in the European Cup of Bakery or Coupe d' Europe de la Boulangerie. We have been friends all these years, and we regularly meet as we work, doing demonstrations in Europe, or as jury members at the Coupe du Monde in Paris.

This very soft brioche has a soft caramelised cream and sugar mixture in the centre with raspberry pieces. The pastry is masked, dusted and garnished with fresh mint and raspberry. The complete recipe and method for this pasty will feature in my next book, The Global Master Bakers Cook Book, scheduled for release about Eastertime 2021.

37. Strawberry Chocolate Twist

The Strawberry Chocolate Chocolatine Twist made similar to the Coupe Du Monde Chocolatine recipe on page 123, but with strawberry chocolate home-made bars. There is a video in other resources on how to make the bars and form the pastry. The pastry is garnished after baking and cooling with strawberry powder, icing sugar, a red isomalt disc of bubble sugar, and a 1/4 strawberry brushed with apricot jam. I filled macaron silicone shapes with the red infused isolalt powder and baked it until it began to bubble. This pastry is simply delicious served warm with whipped fresh cream and fresh strawberries when strawberries are in season and at their most flavoursome. Try it warm with a dust of icing sugar and of course even more strawberries to finish it off with a coffee or afternoon tea.

38. Nutella Cruffin Style Pastry

The cruffin was originally created by Kate Reid of Lune Croissanterie in Melbourne, Australia, in 2013. A Cruffin is a hybrid of a croissant and muffin. Cruffin-style pastries are popular and easily made from croissant pastry on page 52. The pastry block is opened out before sheeting, dredged with sugar, refolded, sheeted to 4 mm, and cut into strips of approx to make them extra crunchy. 3 cm wide and 25 cm long.

You can see how I form the pastry in the resources section and place them into high steel rings to proof and bake. Before baking and after proofing, I dredge them with castor sugar using a small sieve to help caramelise the pastry more during the bake. After baking, they are cooled, filled with Nutella and garnished with a light dust of icing sugar. The steel ring sizes I used were 60 mm high and 70 mm across. Wilton's make a special deep muffin shape for cruffins. Each shape has six indentations for perfect Cruffins. Ensure you butter the tins well and dredge them in sugar before proofing the pastry in them. You can use a range of jams, curds, custards, ganache and other fillings to fill and make a beautiful selection of these pastries.

Home Bakers' Sheeting Hack

Many home bakers struggle with rolling pastry evenly when they first make the laminated pastry by hand. If the pastry is rolled unevenly, the pastry will be of different weights/thicknesses. The underlying layers suffer, causing a lack of volume, poor internal texture, and misshaped baked pastries. If the pastry is thick on one side and thin on the other, the thin side will colour more rapidly in the oven than the thick side and may burn, ruining the product. A nifty hack uses rulers, or wooden batons/lats, which can be purchased at your local hardware store. They come in numerous thicknesses and can be cut to size for you in many stores which offer wood cutting services. I would recommend two sizes to start, 3.5 mm and 4 mm.

Additionally, you need a long rolling pin that extends well beyond the pastry's width and the wooden guides. I have made a YouTube video on rolling the pastry with the wooden guides, and I have inserted the link below. I hope you find it useful.

Hand lamination hack using wooden guides https://youtu.be/fyRCB4G4-Qo

Appendix - A – Materials and Methods

Materials and Methods

Optional Raw Materials Used In The Process

Spelt Croissant Dough	**Spelt Chocolate Dough**
➢ Spelt flour	Spelt flour
➢ Fresh full-fat milk	Fresh full-fat milk
➢ Filtered water	Filtered water
➢ Castor sugar	Castor sugar
➢ Skimmed milk powder	Skimmed milk powder
➢ Osmotolerant yeast	Osmotolerant yeast
➢ Barley malt liquid	Barley malt liquid
➢ Salt	Salt
➢ Butter Kerrygold	Butter Kerrygold
➢ Butter dry	Butter dry

➢ **Additional Ingredients, Garnishes And Fillings:**

- ➢ Cocoa powder
- ➢ Croissant chocolate bars
- ➢ Candied orange segments
- ➢ Candied orange batons

Details of many ingredient product specifications and their suppliers' list can be found in the appendices at the end of this publication.

The Equipment, Small Tools and Other Items Required In The Pastry Kitchen

1. Wedderburn DS-575 digital weighing scales, with current calibration certificate accurate 16 kg to 2 g and stainless-steel ingredient bowls for scaling the ingredients.

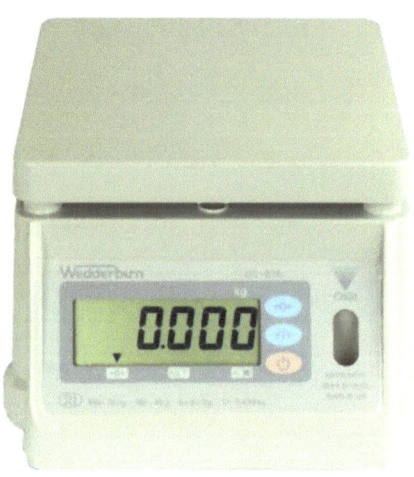 

2. Alla France® calibrated digital infrared thermometer- temperature range – 50 to + 380°C for measuring dough water and pastry temperature.

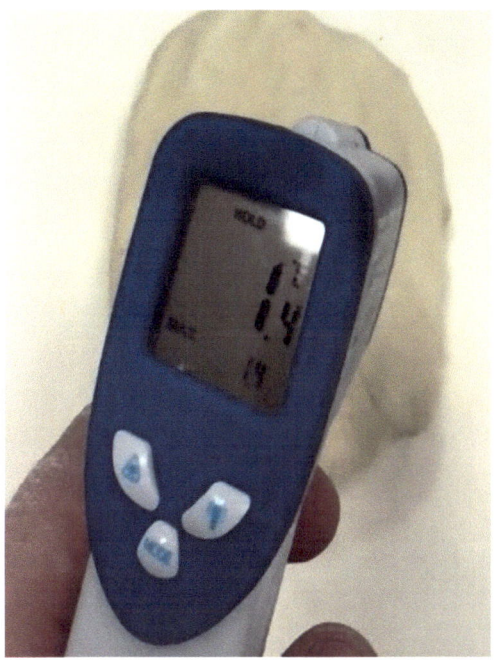

3. Dough mixer – Hobart – 20qt with dough hook and beater attachment

4. Rondo pastry sheeter for rolling and sheeting pastry and a water spray bottle for merging pastry

5. Freezer & refrigerator fitted with shelving space

6. High-speed blast freezer or Cryopack® ice blankets

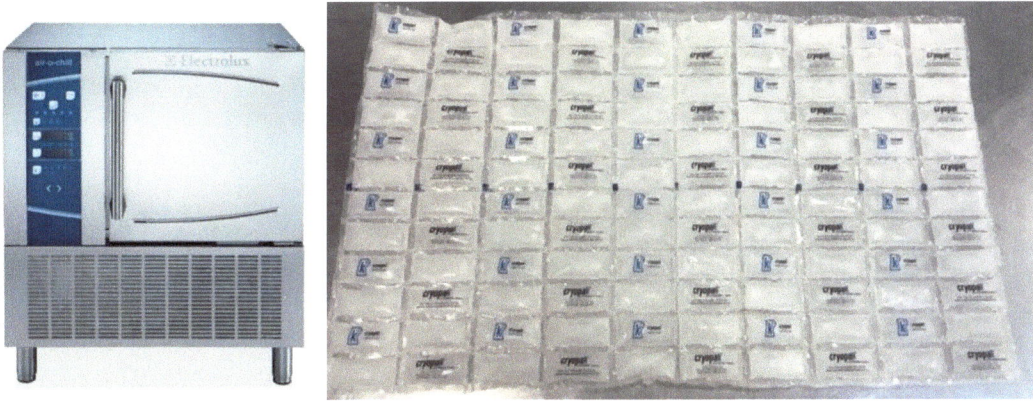

7. Aluminium trays and silicone lining paper for the pastry, used in the freezer, proofing cabinet and oven

8. Makeup and cutting table with refrigerated under storage – stainless steel - Inox

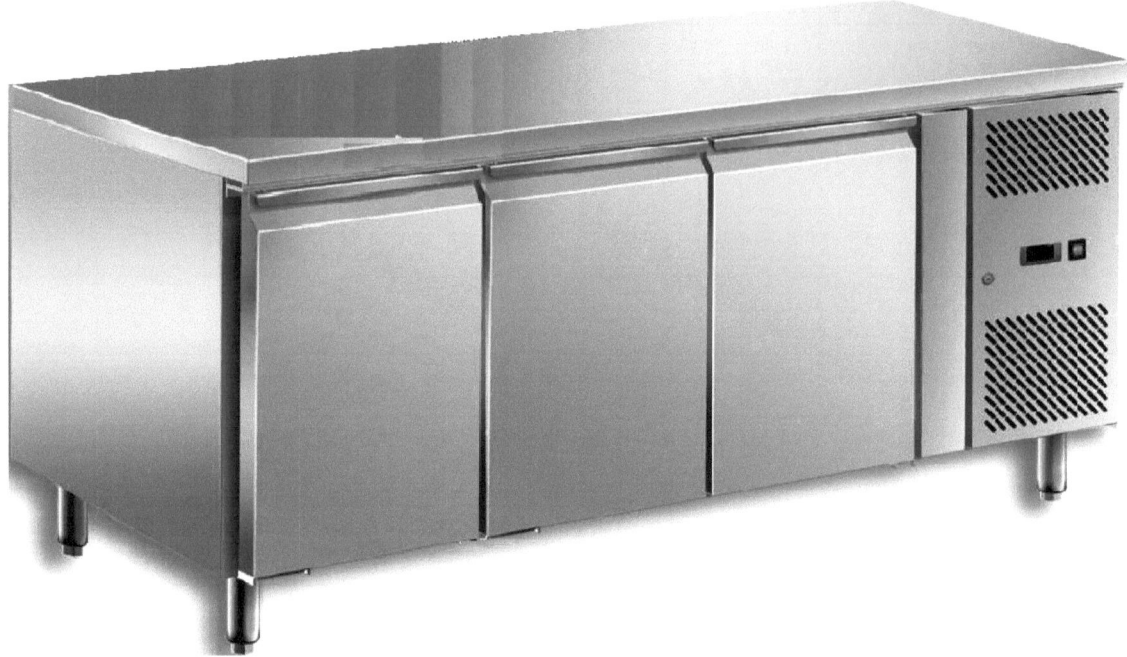

9. Proofing cabinet capable of maintaining 75% –85% humidity and capable of consistently maintaining 25 °C –28 °C (this is a *critical* maximum temperature) as the butter will run out of the layers if the cabinet gets any hotter.

10. Sveba Dahlen Rack oven and electric Deck oven, Sveba Dalen/Tom Chandley.

11. Cooling wires

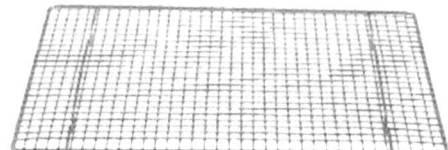

Ingredient Storage

- Stainless steel shelving and plastic food grade containers for storing flour, salt, cocoa, sugar, chocolate bars, orange pieces and all dry ambient ingredients.
- Walk-in or reach-in refrigerator for butter, milk and dough storage to include shelving.

Weighing Station

- Weighing station table
- Recipe book holder if available
- Ingredient holders and dispensers for salt, milk powder, sugar, spelt flour, cocoa, and other items.
- Digital weighing scales x 1-16 kg capacity precision 1g
- Scoops x 6
- Jug 1 x 1L; Jug 1 x 2L
- Flour sieve

Mixing Station

- Digital infrared thermometer for measuring dough temperature
- Hobart mixer 10 qt capacity with a dough hook

Dough Storage Containers

- Plastic dough containers and stainless-steel racks

Lamination Station

- Pastry sheeter free standing-1150 cm×60 cm pastry belts
- Large rolling pin×1; small rolling pin×1
- Measuring tape/ruler/templates
- Water spray gun

Makeup Table and Small Tools

- Four-wheel pastry dividers × 1
- French knife–25 cm; Trimming knife–10 cm
- Bench scraper
- Plastic scraper
- Pastry brush
- Digital weighing scales×1–Capacity 6 kg–precision 1 g

Trollies and Baking Trays

- 30 × 18–inch baking trays; 15 × 18–inch baking trays
- 16–space stainless steel rack

Freezing Equipment

- Domestic freezer
- Chest freezer
- Upright freezer
- Walk-in freezer
- Blast freezer if available
- Ice blankets

Packaging Station for Sales and Distribution

- Racking for storage of wrapping and packaging equipment
- Paper bags for 1–2 units
- Cardboard packaging boxes, for 1, 4–& 6–units ambient sale
- Cardboard boxes 35 cm×45 cm for wholesale sales of 50 frozen units
- Plastic liners for cardboard boxes
- Packaging tape dispensers
- Product label blanks
- PC station for label printing of products

Ingredients and Contact Details

Materials and Methods

Many of the ingredients used in viennoiserie production are available globally. However, there can be issues sourcing ingredients from other companies. I am providing information in this chapter on the ingredient specifications and obtaining them in Europe. If you live in another part of the world, you can compare the specifications of the ingredients provided in this resource to compare and contrast. You may not get exactly the same, but you should find similar products to help you make great pastry. Follow the links for more information.

Spelt *(Triticum spelta)* Flour:

Appearance: Fine powder/quality cereals

Odour: Free from mustiness and foreign odours

Taste: Mildly nutty flavour free from any rancidity

Additives: If required the flour or cereal is to be produced in accordance with relevant legislation

Raw flour product to be acceptable under Irish legislation specifically; The Bread & Flour Regulation 1998 & Amendments

Storage: 3 months for wholemeal stone ground

Storage: 6 months for white spelt flour

Source:
http://www.vvrsaustralia.com.au/wp-content/uploads/2013/02/Spelt-flour-300x224.jpg

Spelt can be used as the main ingredient in croissant recipes. When the liquid component is added to the spelt flour and mixed, the starch and the two proteins that are naturally occurring in the flour absorb water and swell; this is known as hydrating the flour. The two proteins, gliadin and glutenin, combine in the dough when hydrated to form the protein called gluten (The Baking Industry Research Trust, 2016). The gluten gives the dough the properties it requires to form an elastic matrix that can trap the CO_2 gases given off as a by-product of yeast fermentation. The trapped gases and the elastic protein matrix are responsible for the light, airy structure of the crumb of yeasted baked goods.

Whole Milk

Total solids (% m/m) Min 12.0% Milk
Butterfat (% m/m) 3.5 – 4.0%
MSNF (% m/m) 8.5 – 9.0 %
Specific gravity min 1.030
Phosphatase (p-nitro phenol) <10ug/ml <10ug/ml
Antibiotics negative
pH 6.7 ± 0.2 6.7 ± 0.2
Appearance Free from burn particles, foreign and extraneous matter
Colour creamy white Free from chemicals and other flavours. Clean milk flavour. Temperature (°C) Less than °1C max 6 °C

Source: http://strathroy.lairdev.com/wp-content/uploads/2011/11/goats_milk_01.jpg

Milk is one of the moistening and enriching agents used to make pastry dough. Water and egg are also commonly used. Milk contributes towards a softer eating product, and the natural sugar present in the milk improves crust colour.

Castor or Granulated Sugar

Food grade: Free from contamination, mould growth or microbial spoilage
Appearance: White crystallised granules free from clumps or damp
Colour: Shiny with a highly reflective surface; free from impurities
Flavour: Tastes sweet of sugar with a rich flavour
Aroma -N/A
Storage; Store in a cool dry place away from contaminants in a sealed container
Shelf life: Indefinite (Best before end date usually three years after packaging)
Variety: Gem

Source: http://www.conatycatering.com/image/cache/data/01105506-500x500.jpg

Sugar contributes sweetness and enrichment to the dough. Sugar is also a food source for the yeast and assists the yeast, by feeding it, to operate in a high-fat environment. Sugar contributes towards a softer eating product, imparts sweetness and has a significant role in the pastry's colour during the baking process.

Milk Powder

Manufactured from fresh pasteurized milk. A white to slightly yellowish, free-flowing powder. Taste is clean slightly sweet, milky and neutral with no distinctive off-flavours. No neutralising materials, additives or preservatives product packed in multiwall Kraft paper bag with poly liner can be stored in dry cool conditions (below 25 °C and 70 % Rh) for 1 year.

Source: https://kerrygold.com/products/kerrygold-full-cream-milk-powder/

Milk powder improves both crumb and crust colour in the dough and contributes towards a softer eating baked product.

Barley Liquid Malt (Non-Diastatic)

Appearance: A viscous liquid amber or yellowish brown in colour (Free from any adulterants, off odour, foreign flavour and impurities)
Identification: Positive for Carbohydrates
Taste: Characteristic Malt and sweet taste free from any detectable foreign or off flavour i.e. not be sharp or bitter or sour tail

Source: https://www.meridianfoods.co.uk/Products/Other-ranges/Natural-Sweeteners/Organic/Organic-Barley-Malt-Extract

Non-diastatic malt contributes towards the rich chestnut colour of the pastry and is also a food source for the yeast, maintaining dough stability during the cold fermentation process.

Compressed Yeast

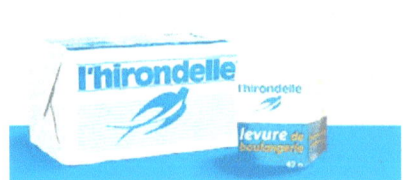

Supplier: Lesaffre
Group: Baker's yeast L'hirondelle (Swift)
Pack Size: 10 kg 10 x 500g
Pack Type: Box
Product Form: Solid
Product Colour: Grey
Shelf life 35 days when stored at 1 °C–4 °C

Source: https://lesaffre.uk/products/compressed-yeast/

Baker's yeast or Saccharomyces cerevisiae is the biological raising agent used to provide raising of the pastry. The by-product of yeast fermentation - CO_2 is trapped by the gluten matrix and coupled with the mechanical lamination of the butter layers in the dough, provide the pastry with its light and airy structure as the gas expands, trapped by the gluten matrix in the oven during baking causing the pastry to rise

Salt

Iodized Salt is dried, sieved, edible and iodized for human consumption
Sodium chloride as NaCl: minimum 97.0 % (on dry matter)
Moisture content: max 3.0% (m/m)
Water insoluble matter: max 0.2 % (m/m)
Iodine: 30.0 – 50.0 mg/kg (means 50 – 84mg of potassium iodate per kg of salt)
Colour: shall be white and 10g of salt in 100ml water shall give a colourless solution having a neutral reaction. Store under dry, ventilated and hygienic conditions

Source: http://fyi.uwex.edu/safepreserving/files/2014/08/salt.jpg

Salt has an astringent effect on the gluten formed in the dough. Salt also helps to control the fermentation of the yeast and imparts colour to the finished baked dough.

Butter

Food grade: free from contamination, rancidity, mould growth or microbial spoilage. Sourced from grass-fed cows. Made with pasteurized cream and salt. Milk fat 80% moisture max. 18.2% and milk solid non-fat max. 1.8%, No trans-fat, No hormones
No artificial colours or ingredients No added vegetable oil. Butter has a shelf life of around 3 months for unsalted and 5 months for salted butter. Keep refrigerated at + 3°C.

Source: http://kerrygold.com/images/sized/images/uploads/KG_Pure_Irish_Butter-604x414.png

Butter enriches the croissant dough, the natural beta carotene adding colour to both the crust and the crumb. Butter shortens the dough and imparts both flavour and colour to the overall dough. This butter also lubricates the gluten and is added to the dough at the mixing stage for this purpose.

Dry Butter

Food grade: free from contamination, rancidity, mould growth or microbial spoilage
Pasteurised cream (manufactured from cow milk), lactic ferments
Milk fat 84%, moisture max. 14.6% and milk solid non-fat max. 1.8%. No colour or additives
Butter has a shelf life of around 3 months for unsalted and 5 months for salted butter. Store in a freezer.
When in use, keep refrigerated at + 3−8°C max

Source: https://pro.elle-et-vire.com/en/products/butters/extra-dry-butter-84-fat

Butter enriches the croissant dough and pastry, the natural beta carotene adding colour to both the crust and the crumb. Butter shortens the dough and imparts both flavour and colour to the overall dough. This butter is also drier than the Kerrygold butter used in the dough making and is specially designed for the lamination process. The lamination butter is rolled and folded into the dough, building up tiny dough and butter layers. The butter separates the dough as it is folded, generating an independent film that enables these alternating layers of dough and butter to form. The lamination is the building block of the pastry and is referred to as mechanical aeration. It is the second of two types of aeration used to achieve aeration in the pastry and imparts a light, flaky property to the finished pastry.

Cocoa Powder

Food grade: free from contamination, rancidity, mould growth or microbial spoilage
Appearance: Dry fine brown powder free from clumps (Very similar to heavy cornflour)
Colour: Dark brown with an unreflective appearance; free from impurities
Flavour: Tastes of chocolate however has a tendency to be more astringent and bitter
Aroma – Chocolate aroma
Storage; Store in a cool dry place away from contaminants in a sealed container
Shelf life: Indefinite (Best before end date usually three years after packaging)
Sole Producer; Barry Callebaut (Produced under licence)
Other Notes; Free from dairy (Lactose)

Source: http://foodie-isms.com/wp-content/uploads/2011/04/cocoa-powder.jpg

Cocoa powder is used to provide colour and flavour to the dough using a natural product. In this instance, the cocoa powder is mixed with the laminating butter in advance of the laminating process; a butter block is made and incorporated into the dough. When used in this fashion, the chocolate butter not only provides flavour and colour, it also gives the pastry a unique aspect or look, differentiating it from other products in this class of pastry.

Cocoa as a functional ingredient in chocolate laminating dough

Chocolate Croissant Batons

300 pieces Cardboard carton // 15 Cardboard cartons per case
Cacao Barry
Comments: Easy, fast, and formulated to be baked. For filling Viennese pastry like pain au chocolat.
Specifications,
Storage Conditions: Dry and cool (68–72°F, 20–22°C)
Shelf Life (months):12.0
Ingredients: Sugar, cocoa liquor, cocoa butter, emulsifier: soya lecithin, vanillin flavour
Additional Notes: Sugar: 54% Cocoa mass: 44% Store in a dry place, away from foreign odours and protected from direct sunlight.

Source: https://www.cacao-barry.com/en-CA/chocolate-couverture-cocoa/chd-bb-308by/extruded-batons-boulangers

The chocolate bars for making pain au chocolat are specially made and tempered chocolate pieces specifically designed not to burn in the oven when subjected to heat. Their primary function is the provision of flavour in the product.

Candied Orange Segments

A firm, whole candied orange slice with a punchy citrus flavour combined with a natural sweet structure. Perfect for enrobing with chocolate. A natural product without sulphites. Storage Conditions: Dry and cool (68 °F –72°F, 20 °C –22°C). Shelf Life (months):18.0 Store in a dry place, away from foreign odours and protected from direct sunlight.

Source: https://www.keylink.org/product/candied-orange-slices-drained

The candied orange segments are garnishes designed to reflect the flavour of the product. The candied orange segments are added after baking and cooling for decorative purposes. They are a natural product free of sulphides.

Candied Orange Batons

Premium candied orange strips are dark and firm with an intense orange aroma which can be enrobed or dipped in chocolate. A natural product without sulphites.

Storage Conditions: Dry and cool (68–72°F, 20–22°C). Shelf Life 18 months.

Store in a dry place, away from foreign odours and protected from direct sunlight.

Source: https://www.keylink.org/product/candied-straight-orange-peel-strips-drained-1

The candied orange bars are a filling designed to enhance the flavour of the product. The candied orange segments are added before baking for flavouring purposes. They are a natural product, free of sulphides.

Appendix - B – Pre Fermented Croissant Dough Hand Lamination

39. Hand Laminated Croissant 50 % Preferment & Sourdough Levain

Hand Laminated Croissant 50% Preferment + Levain

Ingredients	1 MIX	1/2 mix	Bakers %	Hydration %
	g	g	767	55.11
Preferment Stage 1 Overnight 14-16 hrs				
Strong Flour	368	184	48.0 %	
Water	205	103	26.7 %	
Yeast	0.5	0.25	0.1 %	
Total	574		74.8 %	
Sourdough addition dough stage day 1				
Water	30	15	3.9 %	
Flour	30	15	3.9 %	
Sourdough	15	8	2.0 %	
Sourdough starter 1 : 2 : 2	75	38	9.8 %	
Dough Stage day 2				
Preferment stage	574	287	74.8 %	
Sourdough stage	75	38	9.8 %	
Strong Flour	368	184	48.0 %	
Milk	180	90	23.5 %	
Sugar	96	48	12.5 %	
Yeast fresh	29	15	3.8 %	
Milk powder	18	9	2.3 %	
Barley malt extract (non diastatic)	15	8	2.0 %	
Salt	13	7	1.7 %	
Butter	38	19	5.0 %	
Dough head weight	1,331	665	Butter on Dough %	Total Butter % in both Dough & Lamination
Lamination Stage				
Laminating butter	335	168	25.2	30.1
Total batch weight	1,666	833		
Yield	22	11		
Scaling wt in grams	75			

I regularly engage with international bakers of all proficiency levels in online platforms such as Facebook and Instagram, assisting them with problems and trying to help them achieve improved results in laminated pastry making. One of the most consistent issues I identified from these platforms were those who hand-laminated. Pastry elastic recoil presented problems for many while hand-rolling, so I have formulated a special new recipe to address this. I have test baked several times, adjusting the preferment, hydration and the work sequence. The result is a very pleasant tasting pastry, which hand rolls extremely well due to the dough's increased hydration, overnight pre-fermentation and use of sourdough.

The flour used by bakers in different countries varies greatly. In Canada for example, patent flour can be very strong with protein levels typically 10.0% –12.5% (12.8% –14.5% dry basis) and an ash content of: 0.35% – 0.55% (0.41% – 0.64% dry basis). My learned Canadian friend, colleague Alan Dumonceaux (CDM) and world masters Viennoiserie candidate recommended a preferment technique for those who only had very strong flour available to them. This process is a two-day process, where, day 1, a preferment is made, the sourdough is added, and the dough is fermented overnight at room temperature 18 °C –22 °C. Day 2, the preferment is mixed into a dough and the remaining 50% of the flour and the rest of the ingredients. The dough was mixed using a KitchenAid™ stand mixer for 3 minutes on slow and 3 minutes on medium speed using a dough hook. The dough is fermented at room temperature for 45 minutes, then degassed, rolling it out using a rolling pin into a rectangle, placed on a tray, covered with plastic and chilled for 2 hours in a refrigerator until the dough is at a temperature of 3 °C –4 °C. The butter block should be prepared at this time and placed in the refrigerator until required.

The dough is then taken from the refrigerator along with the butter block. I used the **3-4-3** system for croissant and the **3-4-4** system for pain au chocolat. The lock-in is performed, and it is possible to give the dough all its turns together, providing the room and surfaces you work on are relatively cool. I recommend that the make-up is staggered in warm climates, placing the pastry back to chill for 30 minutes in a refrigerator or freezer until cool enough to work. The pastry may need a little bit of extra dusting flour when processing. When all the turns are completed, and the pastry is ready to process, sheet as normal, cut, shape and proof. The pastry will be quite active, and I noticed that the croissants and pain au chocolat will proof quicker than normal.

The science behind this method is to make an overnight preferment using 50% of the flour in the recipe and let the enzymes do most of the work on the gluten during fermentation. As many of the bakers online also bake sourdough, I added just under 10% sourdough to the recipe, adding extra flavour and extensibility to the dough. The protease degrades the protein overnight during the fermentation process, which greatly improves extensibility and makes the dough a pleasure to roll. I have made the recipe with up to 57% hydration (using a 13% extra-strong bakers' flour), but I found that the wetter dough required a lot more dusting flour and was quite sticky and not too easy to handle. My recommendation is to use approximately 52%–55% hydration. Have fun, everyone!

Jimmy G.

Other Online Resources

My YouTube Channel https://www.youtube.com/channel/ucsmfbyjsiu4e7du-kmu6ing/

Twisted chocolatine shaping using homemade chocolate bars

https://youtu.be/klsvyc1omoo

Pain chocolate shaping - Three ways https://youtu.be/uheq8fjbffk

Croissant bicolor 3-4-4 pastry process https://youtu.be/q-o0cyjane0

Twisted chocolatine bicolor shaping and makeup https://youtu.be/qr_SS3aWSRs

Slicing laminated pastry to relieve elastic recoil https://youtu.be/gscqic8hpxk

Croissant make up dough video with rolling and a 3 fold https://youtu.be/nhsavshz6c0

Explaining elastic recoil tension in laminated pastry https://youtu.be/vi90mhc2t_U

The lock in process of dough and butter in pastry making https://youtu.be/J_j4umea7ow

Butter block and hand lamination https://youtu.be/KI7VTQQISFw

Coupe du Monde Chocolatine Toulouse, France 2019 https://youtu.be/HQW4TfDnmvY

Chocolatine scored using a claw and scored using a knife https://youtu.be/s-aV1bzKnpc

Raspberry pear marinade, dusting and masking techniques

https://youtu.be/qYUHmcZbypU

How to incorporate trimmings to reduce wastage https://youtu.be/mA22qWphP8E

The correct procedure for wrapping laminated pastry https://youtu.be/RAb-aVWX6tQ

Making frozen Crème Pâtissière pieces for viennoiserie https://youtu.be/kwUZEcjtak4

How to insert frozen Crème Pâtissière into proofed pastry https://youtu.be/NBm1Ti-YAWU

Christmas jiggle jiggle https://youtu.be/2ifa63fspqs

Christmas chocolatines https://youtu.be/bxzinvf118e

Seaweed dissertation: https://arrow.tudublin.ie/tfschcafdis/1/

™ style pastries: https://youtu.be/yturuzkkmdc

5-4-3 Hand lamination sourdough croissant pastry: https://youtu.be/irmbjlvxls4

Chilling laminated dough using frozen vegetables https://youtu.be/-WZ9w0gPjyg

Brød &Taylor home proofer: https://brodandtaylor.com/

Hand lamination hack using wooden guides: https://youtu.be/fyRCB4G4-Qo

Kouign Amman preparation final fold: https://www.youtube.com/watch?v=gNM22D7jLhY

Puff Pastry Hand Lamination Bible: https://youtu.be/rKvDjMQDySY

Christmas Mince Pies made with Butter Puff Pastry: https://youtu.be/qJN_Qbf9ZNM

Hand rolling a croissant: https://youtu.be/VoeUD3wwRQ0

References

Arat, E., 2019. *The History of Turkish Coffee.* https://www.turkishcoffeeworld.com/History-of-Coffee-s/60.htm, last access 2019-11-19.

Bramen, L., 2010. *When Food Changed History: The French Revolution.* Https://www.smithsonianmag.com/arts-culture/when-food-canged-history-the-french-revolution-93598442/, last access 2019-11-19.

Chevallier, J. 2009. *August Zang and the French Croissant: How Viennoiserie came to France.* 2nd ed. North Hollywood (California), Chez Jim Books.

Culinary Institute of America. 2016. *Baking and Pastry.* Hoboken (New Jersey), John Wiley & Sons.

City of Vienna, 2019. *1683 - the beginning of Viennese coffee house culture.* Https://www.wien.gv.at/english/culture-history/viennese-coffee-culture.html, last access 2019-11-19.].

Fiegl, A., 2015. *Is the Croissant really French - A brief history of the croissant – from kipfel to Cronut?* Https://www.smithsonianmag.com/arts-culture/croissant-really-french-180955130/, last access 2019-11-19.

Goldstein D, Mintz S. 2015. *The Oxford Companion to Sugar and Sweets.* Oxford, Oxford University Press.

Hartings, M., 2016. *Chemistry in Your Kitchen.* Cambridge, The Royal Society of Chemistry.

Labensky SR, Martel P, Van Damme E. 2009. *On Baking.* 2nd ed. Columbus (Ohio), Pearson Prentice Hall.

NIIR Board of Consultants & Engineers. 2014. *The Complete Technology Book on Bakery Products (Baking Science with formulation and production).* 3rd ed. Deli, NIIR Project Consultancy Services.

Pastry Chef Central. 2019. *Puff Pastry Dough.* https://www.pastrychef.com/Puff-Pastry-Dough_ep_70.html, last access 2019-11-19.

Peterson, J., 2012. *Baking.* Berkeley (California), Potter/tenspeed/Harmony.

Willan, A., 2016. *Oxford Reference: France.* Http://www.oxfordreference.com/view/10.1093/acref/9780199313396.001.0001/acref-9780199313396-e-202 last access 2019-11-19.

BakerPedia, 2020. *Croissant.* [Online]
Available at: https://bakerpedia.com/processes/croissant/
[Accessed 8 April, 2020].

Bakerpedia, n.d. *Puff Pastry.* [Online]
Available at: https://bakerpedia.com/processes/puff-pastry/
[Accessed 8 April, 2020].

Berry, D. R., Russell, I. & Stewart, G., 2012. *Yeast Biotechnology.* 3 ed. NY(NY): Springer.

Brown, A. C., 2018. *Understanding food: principles and preparation.* 6th ed. Manoa(Hawaii): Cengage Learning.

Calvel, R., 2001. *The Taste of Bread.* s.l.:Springer.

Cauvain, S. P., 2017. *Baking Problems Solved.* 1 ed. Cambridge: Woodhead Publishing.

Chevallier, J., 2009. *August Zang and the French Croissant: How Viennoiserie Came to France.* 2nd ed. Northwood(California): Chez Jim Books.

Doves Farm, 2020. *European flour numbering system.* [Online]
Available at: https://www.dovesfarm.co.uk/hints-tips/cheat-sheets/european-flour-numbering-system
[Accessed 17 May, 2020].

Goldstein, D. & Mintz, S., 2015. *The Oxford Companion to Sugar and Sweets.* Oxford: Oxford University Press.

Griffin, J., 2016. *Chocolatine Time-lapse Video YouTube,* Galway: s.n.

Griffin, J. A., 2015. *An Investigative study into the beneficial use of seaweed in bread and the broader food industry.* Dublin: James A. Griffin.

Griffin, J. A., 2015. *One-minute croissant butter block technique,* Galway: James Griffin.

Griffin, J. A., 2016. *Pain au Chocolat "Wobble" Test,* Galway: James Griffin.

Haegens, N. n.d. *Puff pastry and Danish pastry.* [Online]
Available at: http://www.classofoods.com/page4_1.html
[Accessed 08 April, 2020].

Hutkins, R., 2008. *Microbiology and Technology of Fermented Foods.* Hoboken(New Jersey): John Wiley & Sons.

Jason Davies, 2020. *jasondavies.com*. [Online]
Available at: https://www.jasondavies.com/wordcloud/
[Accessed 20 March, 2020].

Labensky, S. R., Martel, P. & Van Damme, E., 2009. *On Baking.* 2nd ed. Columbus(Ohio): Pearson Prentice Hall.

Lonely Planet Food, 2017. *From the Source - France: Authentic Recipes From the People That Know Them ....* 1 ed. Wilson(Wyoming): Lonely Planet Food.

NIIR Board of Consultants and Engineers, 2014. *The Complete Technology Book on Bakery Products (Baking Science with formulation and production).* 3rd ed. Deli: Niir Project Consultancy Services.

Ranken, M., Baker, C. G. .. & Kill, R. eds., 1997. *Food Industries Manual.* 24 ed. Padstow(Cornwall): Springer.

Rodriguez, B. M. & Merangioni, A. G., 2018. *Physics Today,* 1(70), p. 71.

Rondo, n.d. *Rondo Dough-how and more,* Burgdorf: s.n.

Stamm, M., 2011. *The Pastry Chef's Apprentice: An Insider's Guide to Creating and Baking Sweet confections and pastries taught by the masters.* Beverly(MA): Quarry Books.

The Baking Industry Research Trust, 2016. *What Role Does Gluten Play In Bread Making?.* [Online]
Available at: http://www.bakeinfo.co.nz/Facts/Gluten/What-role-does-gluten-play-in-bread-making-
[Accessed 1 May, 2016].

The Culinary Institute of America, 2016. *Baking and Pastry.* Hoboken(New Jersey): John Wiley & Sons.

Vernet, S., 2020. *French Croissants,* Montpellier: s.n.

Weekendbakery.com, 2020. *Understanding flour types.* [Online]
Available at: https://www.weekendbakery.com/posts/understanding-flour-types/
[Accessed 17 May, 2020].

Willan, A., 2016. *Oxford Reference: France.* [Online]
Available at:
http://www.oxfordreference.com/view/10.1093/acref/9780199313396.001.0001/acref-

9780199313396-e-202

[Accessed 16 January, 2016].

Yankellow, J., 2005. *Lamination: Layers beyond imagination,* San Francisco: s.n.

The Art of Lamination Index

Lamination systems

3-3-3-3-system, 68
3-4-3 system, 53
5-4-3 system, 61
3-4-4 system, 65
3-fold, 4, 18, 62
4-leaf clover design, 121, 123

A
Additional ingredients, 147
Additional Notes, 163
African Bakery Cup, 81
Air, 78, 111
Air spaces, 59–60, 87
Alignment, 26, 104
Almond Cream Recipe, 5, 80
Almond Twice-Baked Croissant, 5, 79
Alternating dough/butter/dough layers, 52
  forming long thin, 16
Alternating layers, 51–52, 57, 62, 161
  separate, 68
America, 3, 19–20
American flour's ash content, 19
Apple, 106, 119, 138
Apple Pistachio/Apple Raspberry, 6, 138
Apricot jam, 131, 138, 143
  boiled, 135
Aroma, 158, 162
Artisan Baking, 3, 19
Ash, 7, 19, 21
Ash content, 19, 167
Australia, 21, 144

Author, Jimmy Griffin, 1

B
Bacteria, 33–34
Bags, 156, 159
Bake, 31, 38–41, 47, 107, 111, 113, 118, 131, 133, 135–40, 144
Baked goods, 39, 102
Bakeries, 7, 9, 15, 28, 32, 39, 43, 74, 142
Bakers, 1, 3, 12, 18, 22–23, 27, 39, 41–43, 81, 167, 173
  home, 18, 37, 43–44, 47
Bakers flour, 21, 32
Baker's yeast, 160
Baking, 3, 5, 17–18, 23–24, 38–41, 46, 77–78, 119, 123–24, 136–38, 140–41, 143–44, 163–64, 171, 173
Baking Industry Research Trust, 157, 173
Baking process, 91, 98, 159
Baking Science, 171, 173
Baking trays, 6, 37, 106, 134–36, 156
Baking viennoiserie, 39–40
Balance, 36, 38, 105
Barley malt liquid, 147
Bars, 138, 143
  candied orange, 97, 164
Base, 15, 75, 113, 129, 134–36, 140
  pastry triangle, 15
Base Recipes, 5, 82, 122–23
Batches, 18, 39, 43
Beater attachment, 94, 149
Bellies, 4, 56, 59–64, 66–68, 73
  pastry block's, 61

pastry's, 68
Bench scraper, 131, 155
Beurrage, 16, 26
Bitter, 159, 162
Block, 16, 59, 71, 81–82, 86, 93, 95, 104, 109, 116
Book, 1–2, 8–9, 11–12, 14, 28, 30, 37–38, 47, 49, 51, 53–55, 104–5, 107
Book fold, 13, 16, 45, 52, 60, 63, 67
Book Turn, 4, 56
Bottom, 16–17, 38–39, 44–45, 54, 62, 75, 77–78, 110, 136–37
Boulangerie competitions, 44
Bowl, 88, 115, 124
Bread, 10, 16, 19, 21, 27–28, 30–31, 34, 40, 55, 102, 172
Brioche, 18, 90, 116, 140
   laminated, 5, 116–18
Brush, 77, 80, 135
Bubble sugar, 124, 143
   orange, 123–24, 126
Burn, 24, 137, 145, 163
Butter, 15–17, 22–26, 29, 42–44, 48–60, 62–65, 67–71, 80, 82–83, 102–3, 112–13, 115–16, 118, 122–24, 128–29, 134, 139–41, 147, 161
   croissant, 26
   dry, 24–25, 161
   salted, 118, 161
Butter-604x414, 161
Butter block, 16–17, 49–50, 52, 54, 62, 69, 103, 107, 109, 115, 162, 167
   seaweed, 103
Butter block and hand lamination https, 169
Butter content, high, 107
Butter croissant pastry, 53

Butter crystals, 25–26
Butter enriches, 161
Butter/fat, 50
Butterfat, 16, 25–26, 158
Butter flavours, 82
Butter Kerrygold, 147
Butter layers, 16, 26, 37, 68, 71, 77, 160–61
Butter pastry, 89
   hand-laminated, 123

C
Canada, 21, 167
Candidates, 121
Candied Orange Batons, 147, 164
Cappuccino Chocolatine, 6, 139
Career, 10, 81
CDM, 7, 167
CDMC. *See* Coupe Du Monde Chocolatine
Centre, 7, 45–46, 54–55, 63, 69–70, 73, 88, 115, 118, 120, 124
Chef Peter Yuen, 1
Chemicals, 33, 158
Chemistry, 171
Children, 10, 50
Chill, 27, 43–45, 60, 64–65, 73, 75, 115, 167
Chilling, 17, 44–45, 170
Chilling pastry, 3, 43, 46
Chocolat, 5, 46, 66, 68, 71, 76, 88, 90, 163, 167–68, 172
Chocolate and Plain Doughs, 84
Chocolate bars, 86, 92, 100–101, 126, 154, 163
Chocolate brioche, 81, 90, 92
Chocolate butter, 69–70, 82–85, 96, 139, 162
Chocolate croissant bar, 96
Chocolate Croissant Batons, 163

Chocolate croissant dough, 93
Chocolate croissant dough highlights, 123–24
Chocolate croissant pastry, 5, 80, 82
Chocolate dough, 90–91, 123, 125, 147
Chocolate dough mix, 124
Chocolate side, 96, 125
Chocolatine, 5, 7, 16, 24, 51, 66, 89–90, 93, 100–101, 124–26, 140
Chocolatine baking, 88
Chocolatine Cutting Guide Table, 4, 75
Christmas Sweet Mince Pies, 170
CIA (Culinary Institute of America), 14, 171, 173
City, 14, 120, 171
CO2 gases, 33–34, 157
Cocoa, 124, 154, 162
Cocoa powder, 69, 82, 90–91, 124, 141, 147, 162
Coils/shoulders, 75
Colour, 20, 23–24, 39, 43, 91, 99, 105, 123–24, 126–27, 145, 159–62
Colour and flavours, 127, 162
Colour Cross Lamination-The Christmas Chocolatine, 5, 99
Commercial electric multi-deck ovens, 39
Competition, 10, 120–21, 125–26
Competitors, 120–21
Components, 25, 42, 50
Compressed yeast, 18, 22, 160
  fresh, 18
Cons, 54, 62, 69
Consistency, 16, 26, 29, 32, 35, 47–48, 58
Consultant, 10, 67, 173
Container, sealed, 127, 158, 162

Contamination, 158, 161–62
Control, 43, 57, 71, 160
Convection ovens, 39–41, 77
Core, 7, 40, 45–46, 87–88
Core temperature, 3, 7, 43, 46, 64, 138
Countries, 21, 39, 47, 167
Coupe, 5, 7–10, 44, 90, 120–22, 142–43, 169
Coupe Du Monde Chocolatine (CDMC), 5, 7, 10, 24, 90, 120–22, 169
Cream
  almond, 80
  chocolatine ice, 121
Creation time, 8
Creativity, 8–9, 81, 122
Creator, iconic bicolour croissant's, 81
Crème pâtissière, 119, 127–28, 134, 136, 138
  frozen, 129, 132–33, 138, 169
Crescent shape, 15
Crispy, 112, 114, 136
Croissant and Chocolatine Cutting Guide Table, 4, 75
Croissant and pain, 46, 76, 88, 104, 168
Croissant dough, 23, 25, 83, 85, 90, 92, 95–96, 108, 134, 140, 147, 161
  hand rolling, 58
  plain, 90, 96
Croissant dough block, 90, 95, 104
Croissant pastry, 29, 46, 50, 65, 81–82, 89, 102, 104, 144
  hand lamination sourdough, 170
  making plain, 70
Croissant recipes, 140, 157

Croissants, 3–4, 14–16, 41–42, 46, 66, 71, 74–76, 97–98, 100, 103–4, 106–7, 138–39, 167–69, 171–72
  almond, 80
  classic, 52, 68
Cruffins, 144
Crumb, 80, 140, 158–59, 161
Crust colour, 158–59
Crystals
  middle-sized, 26
  prime, 26
Culinary Arts, 10, 81
Culinary Institute, 14, 171, 173
Culinary Institute of America. *See* CIA
Cullen, Frank, 9
Custard, 106, 129–30, 144

D
Dark, 19, 124, 162, 164
DDT, 7, 27–28, 118
Deck ovens, 17, 39–40, 77, 83, 104, 106–7, 111, 135
Desired Dough Temperature, 3, 7, 17, 27
Digital weighing scales, 148, 154–55
Dough
  chocolate laminating, 162
  coloured, 86, 91, 100
  coloured/flavoured, 86
  enriched sweet, 16
  finished baked, 160
  high-sugar/high-fat, 23
  incorporating, 55
  no-time, 105
  rich viennoiserie, 118
  separate, 71, 90, 94, 99
  sheeted, 50, 86
  stiffer, 105
  touching, 64
  yeasted, 18
  yeasted brioche, 90, 104
Dough component, 50, 74
Dough heads, 122–23
Dough hook, 134, 149, 154, 167
Dough layers, 50, 54, 56, 58–59
Dough-making water, 18, 34
Dough mixing times, 48
Dough relaxation/fermentation, 60
Dough sheeter, 69, 90
Dough's stickiness, 50
Dough temperature, 18
  final, 27
Dough Touching Points, 4, 7, 50–51, 66, 68
Dough video, 169
Dough weight, 15, 48, 90–91
Doves Farm, 7, 21, 172
Dried yeasts, 18, 22
Dry yeast, active, 18
DTP, 4, 7, 50, 57, 64–65, 68, 71, 86, 139
Dublin, 9–10, 172
Dusting, 124, 131, 138, 169
Dusting flour, 47, 63, 168

E
Edges, 15, 44, 67, 70, 77, 111, 129
Egg, 41–42, 52, 76–77, 80, 106, 112–13, 116, 138, 158
Egg wash, 24, 38, 76–77, 107, 123, 135, 137–38
Egg washing, 5, 17, 52, 76
Elasticity, 22, 30, 36, 48
  good, 22, 48
Elastic recoil tension, 68, 169
Emulsifiers, 18, 163
Enrichment, 117, 159
Equipment, 6, 27, 43, 98, 148

Ets/european-flour-numbering-system, 172
Europe, 3, 10, 18–19, 97, 116, 142, 157
Examples of Cross Lamination Techniques, 93
Experience, 10, 39
Experiment, 81, 113
Extensibility, 23, 168
Extraction rate, 19

F
Fan, 40, 77, 81, 104, 138
Fats, 15, 24, 67
  hard, 16, 25–26
Ferment, 32–34, 107–8
Fermentation, 19, 23, 27, 29–30, 32, 34, 43, 57, 68, 160, 168
  cold, 17, 29
  sourdough's, 33
Fermentation process, cold, 48, 53, 159
Fillings, 86, 91, 106, 113–14, 144, 147
Final fold, 4, 68, 110
Final sheeting, 17, 29, 60–61, 64, 73, 90, 96, 110
Fingers, 49–50, 74, 111, 128
Finish, 135, 138–39
Finishing/packing, 17
Flakier, 74, 81
Flaky, 14, 54, 62, 69, 81, 113
Flavour
  extra, 92, 139, 168
  rich, 113, 158
Flavouring purposes, 97, 164
Flour, 19–22, 27–28, 31–35, 41–42, 47–48, 52–53, 80, 90, 92, 147, 154, 157, 167–68
  all-purpose, 21–22
  baker's, 31–32
  soft pastry type, 22
Flour types, 7, 19–21, 42
Flour weight, total, 41, 107
Fluffy, 80, 128
Folding, 16, 35–36, 52, 56, 61, 66–67, 109
Folds, 1, 4, 7, 13, 16–17, 46, 49–50, 52, 55–56, 59–60, 62–65, 72–74, 105
  half, 16, 50
Fold Sheeting Settings, 4, 60
Food industry, 10, 172
Food Product Development, 10, 81
France, 10, 15, 21, 92, 116, 118, 120, 122, 149, 169, 171–73
Freeze, 44, 71, 127–28
Freezer, 43–44, 52, 54, 57, 64–66, 68, 71, 73, 75, 95, 97, 105–6, 109, 115–16, 150–51
Freezer at-18, 67, 73
Freezer burn, 64, 106
French Croissant, 14, 171–73
French flours, 19–20
Functions, 24, 58, 129

G
Garnishes, 96, 131, 133, 135, 147, 163
Gem, 1, 158
Geraldine, 120
Germany, 9, 20–21, 97
Global Master Bakers Cook Book, 142
Gluten, 29, 57, 68, 157, 160–61, 168
Gluten matrix, 35–36, 160
  dough's, 36
Golden colour, 23, 111
Goldstein, 171–72
Gordon, Kathryn, 9

Great Pastry Making, 3, 22
Griffin, 2, 88, 102, 172
Guide, 3, 20, 75–76
Gummy, 46, 88

H
Hardened butter, 22, 24
Hazelnut, 126, 141
Hearts, 11, 137
Home, 3, 12, 36, 96
Home Bakers' Sheeting Hack, 145
Homemade chocolate bars, 92, 125
Hotter, 32, 77, 152
Https, wooden guides, 145, 170
Humidity, 37–38, 77, 152
   relative, 7, 77, 106, 129, 135
Hydration, 22, 28, 42–43, 47, 112, 167–68
   frozen pastry's, 105
   increased, 47, 167

I
Ice blankets, 17, 43–45, 57, 64–65, 71, 73, 105, 109, 116, 150, 156
Icing sugar, 80, 89, 123–24, 128, 131, 138, 140, 143–44
Increments, 55, 59–60, 63, 67–68
Indentations, 49, 74, 144
Ingredient Choices Used, 3, 22, 51
Ingredients, 3, 6, 22, 27, 32, 35, 41–43, 115–16, 120, 157, 161, 163, 167
Instant coffee butter, 139
Invitation, 120
Ireland, 2, 9–10, 13, 21, 27, 81, 103
Irish flour, 47

J
Jams, 106, 144
Janice, 10–11
Jelly, 38, 77, 88
Jimmyg51, 1–2
Joy, 9, 113, 121
Jury members, 81, 99, 142
   international bakery, 10

K
Kerrygold butter, 161
Keylink Ltd, 97
Kitchens, 12, 37, 171

L
Labensky, 14, 173
Laborde, Geraldine, 120–21
Lactic Acid, 30
Laminate, 54, 107, 115
Laminated Croissant Pastry, 4, 52
Laminated dough, 14, 22, 28, 86, 123, 170
   white, 86
Laminated pastry, 13–16, 18, 24, 30, 35, 44, 47, 49, 81–82, 89, 167, 169
Laminated Pastry Making, 3, 16, 18
Laminated Pastry Production, 3, 17
Laminating pastry, 13
Laminating system, 96, 118
Lamination, 1–2, 4, 7, 12, 22–23, 25, 29, 46, 48–53, 55, 80, 82–83, 93, 102–3, 121–23
   dough head's, 123
   twin, 5, 52, 82
Lamination butter, 26, 43, 94, 103, 134, 161
Lamination Butter Used During Coupe, 24
Lamination layers, 129
Lamination Numbering System, 4, 49
Lamination sequences, 49, 51, 67, 86, 115–17

Lamination systems, 51–52, 58, 107
Lamination techniques, 13, 83
Lamination thickness, 58
Landscape format, 69
Language barriers, 13
Larger machines, 58
Layer Calculation Example, 4, 65
Layer formation, 16, 25
Layering, 63, 72–73, 83
Layers, 16–17, 38, 44, 46–47, 50–52, 54–57, 62–75, 81, 86, 93, 95–96, 100, 108, 115, 123–24, 138–39
  chocolate brioche middle, 140
  crispy, 89
  delicious flaky, 24
  extra, 62
  laminated, 118
  quantity of, 51, 54
  separate, 50, 63–65
  thin, 91
  top, 95
Layer sequences, 72
Leftover croissants, 80
Lesaffre.uk/products/compressed-yeast, 160
Link, 37, 49, 88, 101, 111, 127, 145, 157
Liquid components, 25–26, 157
Liquids, total, 28, 41
Liquid Sourdough Makeup Points, 3, 35
Loading, 40–41, 77
Lock-in, 4, 7, 29, 36, 50, 52, 54–55, 58–59, 61–63, 67–73, 108–9, 115
  5-layer, 17
Lock-In and Lamination Numbering System, 4, 49
Locking, 48, 52
Lock-in number, 49–50, 72
Lock-in phase, 49
Lock-in stage, 62
Luxury, 37, 43
Luxury puff pastry goodies, 114
Lye, 97–98
Lye croissants, 97–98
Lye Dipped Croissant, 5, 97

M
Machine, 20-quart Hobart-type mixing, 53
Make-up process, 16
Malt, 23, 123
Manufacturing process, 24
Market, 18, 81, 91, 105
Martel, 14, 171, 173
Materials and methods, 6, 146–47, 157
Maths, 41, 50
Mature starter culture, 31
Maximum oven spring, 119
Maximum temperature, critical, 152
Melt, 37, 46, 77, 113–14, 119
Mentor, 9
Metal form, special, 125
Metric measures, 12
Microbial spoilage, 158, 161–62
Milk, 14, 42, 113, 116, 128, 154, 158, 161
Milk fat, 161
Milk powder, 53, 154, 159
Mini, required dough temperature, 27
Mix, 32, 34, 41, 52, 94, 107, 115, 124, 128, 134, 140
Mixer, 27, 82, 94, 128, 167
Mixing, 17–18, 20, 23, 27, 48, 52, 90, 108, 118, 121, 124
Mixing times, 17, 53
Mixture, 127–28
Mould growth, 158, 161–62

N
NaOH, 97–98
Natural beta carotene, 161
NIIR Board, 67, 171, 173
Niir Project Consultancy Services, 171, 173
Noribake, 102–3
Number, 4, 7, 13, 15–16, 41, 49–50, 55, 58, 64–65, 74–75, 93
Numbering systems, universal, 49
Numbering system's learning, universal, 49
Numerical value, desired, 16

O
Odour, 157, 159
Ohio, 171, 173
Oil, 24, 29, 46
  orange, 92, 96
Orange chocolate croissant, 96
Orange strips, candied, 126, 164
Oven, 24, 37–41, 74, 77, 98, 105, 130–31, 145, 151, 160, 163
  domestic, 37–38
Oven temperature, 39, 41
Oven Types, 3, 38, 40, 77
Overnight, 17, 31, 108–9, 115, 118
  stored, 109, 115
Overnight fermentation, 52–53, 83, 105
Oxford Reference, 171, 173

P
Pain, 5, 46, 66, 68, 71, 76, 88, 90, 104, 132, 134, 136, 167–68
  making, 66, 163
Palmiers, 110–11
Paris, 1, 8, 10, 14, 44, 142
Pastry, 3–7, 12–13, 15–18, 22–24, 26–27, 29–31, 36–38, 40–41, 43–47, 49–78, 80–83, 86–89, 91–98, 100–101, 103–7, 109–16, 118–19, 129–45, 159–62, 167–69
  bicolor, 52, 82
  egg washing, 77
  expanding, 37
  frozen/pre-proofed, 106
  laminated brioche, 116
  laminated chocolate, 81
  laminated yeasted, 8, 46
  making laminated, 12, 51
  proofed, 46, 119
  raspberry pear, 88
  sheeted, 16, 36, 101, 118
  three-tone, 95
  twin-laminated, 96
Pastry Arts, 11
Pastry baking, 23, 34
Pastry bellies, 59
Pastry block, 29, 35, 44–45, 52, 56–57, 59–64, 67–68, 71, 73, 91, 95
  rotate, 73
Pastry block height, 55, 64
Pastry block production, 74
Pastry centre, proofed, 129
Pastry chills, 45
Pastry dough block, 44
Pastry flour, 21, 80
Pastry flour Stage, 140
Pastry laminating system, 50
Pastry layers, 87
Pastry margarine, 15–16, 53
Pastry recipe, 42, 113, 141
Pastry sheeter, 26, 29, 49, 53, 65, 67, 70, 155
Pastry Sizes/Weight, 4, 74
Pastry's thickness, 45
Pâté fermentée, 24, 48, 125
Patience, 8, 38, 113
Pears, 127, 130, 132–33

baked, 131
Photos, 8, 55, 57, 67, 69–70, 75, 86, 88, 90–91, 116, 118
Place, 25–26, 34–35, 38, 48, 50, 64–66, 71, 73, 76, 78, 94, 107–8, 128–29, 134–36, 138
Plastic, 37, 44, 48, 52–54, 57, 60, 64–65, 67–68, 71, 73, 107–9, 115–16
Plastic bags, 37, 111, 134
Plasticity, 25–26
Plastic liners, 106, 156
Platforms, social media, 10
Pleats, 16, 50, 52, 63, 111
Points, 13, 36, 56, 58, 67, 115, 127
  higher melting, 24–25
Powder/quality cereals, 157
Practice, common, 43
Preferment, 167
  poolish, 48
Pre Fermented Croissant Dough Hand Lamination, 6, 165
Preferment technique, 167
Preparing Chocolate Flavoured Butter, 5, 82
Process, 1, 3, 16–18, 24, 26, 29–30, 33–36, 43–44, 52, 54, 65–69, 83–84, 105, 107–8, 167–69
  freezing, 105–6
Processing, 4, 24, 26, 29, 44, 48, 61, 71, 74, 86, 167
Process Method, 54, 62, 83
Production, 4, 16, 24, 52, 58, 68, 105, 121, 171, 173
Products, 16, 20, 22, 40–41, 77, 81, 83, 97–98, 103, 105, 107, 156–58, 162–64
  bakery, 102, 171, 173
  natural, 97, 162–64
Proof, 37–38, 46–47, 71, 77, 88, 107–8, 133, 136, 138–40, 144, 168

Proof and bake, 71, 133, 136, 139–40, 144
Proofer, 29, 46, 106, 135–36
Proofing, 5, 15, 17, 23, 37–38, 43, 52, 76, 83, 126, 144
Proofing cabinet, 151–52
Proofing pastry, 3, 36–37, 46, 132
Proof stage, 89, 106, 135
Proof time, 17, 77, 135
Puff paste, 14, 16, 74, 109–10, 112–13, 115
  extra flaky, 5, 112–13
Puff pastry, 110, 118, 172

Q
Quality, 21–22, 24, 116
Quantities, 18, 34, 103, 105, 121
Quiche, 113–15

R
Raisins, 5, 46, 51, 68, 88, 116, 134, 136
Ranken, 25, 173
Raspberry butter, 93
Raspberry jam, 130, 133, 138, 140
Raspberry pear marinade, 5, 127, 132, 169
Raspberry pieces, 142
Raspberry powder, 82, 93, 131, 133, 138
Raw flour product, 157
Recipes, 1, 3, 5, 10–12, 22–23, 28, 30–31, 41–43, 105, 107, 112, 114, 121–23, 136, 167–68
Recommended Layering, 4, 74
Rectangle, 52–54, 62, 65, 69, 71, 96, 110, 123, 134, 167
Rectangular shape, 115, 134

Refrigerator, 31, 34–35, 48, 52–53, 71, 80, 83, 105, 107–10, 115–16, 118, 127–28, 134, 167
Release, 33, 35, 56, 59, 62, 134
Resources, 143, 157
  online, 6, 12, 96, 169
Resting, 17, 36, 52, 64, 109, 116
Result, 22, 24, 44–45, 50, 121, 126, 138, 167
Reykjavik, 15
Rollers, 20, 58, 60
Rolling pin, 16, 26, 48, 53, 63, 86, 104, 110, 121, 167
Rondo, 173
Rondo pastry sheeter, 58, 149
Room, 32, 111, 167
Rotate, 29, 35–36, 39, 59–60, 64, 68, 73, 134
Rotate Pastry, 35
Ruining, 91, 145
Rye, 31, 33, 41

S

Sales, 6, 78, 156
Salt, 23–24, 42, 53, 76, 113, 147, 154, 160–61
Sandwich, 16–17, 44, 52
Saucepan, 127–28
Sausage rolls, 112, 114–15
Savoury puff paste recipe, 5, 112
Sequence, 12, 49–50, 73, 83, 90, 115, 139
Set, 20, 40–42, 60, 77, 83, 93, 126–27
Sheet, 48, 58, 63–64, 66, 71, 73, 75, 95, 100, 115–16, 134, 139
  thin, 16, 50, 52, 123
Sheeter, 29, 58–60, 63, 67, 110
Sheeting, 16–17, 45, 48, 52, 54–56, 59–62, 64–69, 73–74, 86, 90, 95, 105, 109–10

Sheeting stage, 36, 66, 134
Sheeting thickness, 72, 75
Shelf life, 24, 78, 158, 160–64
Shrinkage, 29, 68, 75, 109
Sizes, butter block's, 54, 134
Skimmed milk powder, 147
Skin, 43, 98, 128
Skinning, 37, 53–54, 64–65
Slices, 16, 95, 97, 104, 134–36
  candied orange, 92, 96, 163
Slicing, 56, 100, 169
Soggy, 17, 78, 111
Son Dillon, 9
Sourdough, 5, 10, 31–35, 105, 107–8, 167–68
  natural, 107
Sourdough Croissant Production, 107
Sourdough starter, 3, 30, 33, 35
Space, 43, 110, 121
Stage, first, 20, 49, 52, 54, 62
Stages of Preparing Fermented Laminated Pastry, 4, 51
Start, 30, 32, 68, 88, 145
Starter, 30–35, 107
Start rolling, 134, 136
Steps, 4, 15, 19–20, 51, 81
Stick, 24, 63, 100, 104, 138
Storage, 37, 105, 151, 156–58, 162
Strawberry chocolate bars, 101
Strawberry Chocolate Twist, 6, 143
Strawberry powder, 82, 140, 143
Stretch, 35–36, 50, 62
Strips, 63, 93–95, 100, 134, 144
Subject, 1, 13, 105
Sugar, 23, 27, 30, 80, 110, 118–19, 127–28, 136–37, 140, 144, 154, 158–59, 163, 171–72
  natural, 158
Suppliers, 147, 160
Sweet, 114, 122, 141, 159, 171–72

Sweet Puff Paste, 5, 108
System, 4, 13, 51–52, 54, 58, 62, 66, 68–69, 72, 74–75, 93, 96, 167

T
T-45, 22
T-45 Gruau Rouge, 22
T-55, 20, 22
T-65, 22
Table, 3, 6–7, 19–21, 63, 69, 86, 92, 104, 155
Tarwe bloem, 21
Taste, 19, 127, 159, 172
  distinctive, 29
Tastes of chocolate, 162
Tastes sweet of sugar, 158
Team Iceland, 15
Teardrop-shaped cutter, 129, 132
Techniques, 5, 8, 14, 16, 38, 79, 93, 95, 129
Technological University, 10
Temperature, 26–29, 32–34, 37, 40, 44, 46, 48–49, 53, 77, 104, 106, 129, 131
  bakery, 28
  butter's, 43
  pastry's, 49, 57
Tension, elastic, 55–56, 59
Texture, 24, 26, 29, 81, 123, 126
  internal honeycomb, 123
  leafy honeycomb, 62
Thickness, 16–17, 20, 52, 55, 58, 60–61, 63, 66–68, 71, 73, 104, 110
Thinner, 45, 58–59, 75
Thumb, 27–28
Tins, 38, 41, 144
Tip, 15, 71, 132
Top, 15–16, 24, 39–40, 44, 46, 62, 75, 77–78, 80, 90, 93–95, 100, 110, 113, 135–39

Toppings, 119, 138
Touching, 44–45, 56, 64
Touching points, 50, 55–56, 68
Toulouse, 10, 120–21
Trays, wire, 78, 98
Trifold, 65, 71, 73
Trollies, 6, 156
Twin, 81–82, 86, 89
Twin Lamination Croissant, 5, 80
Twin Lamination Pastry, 5, 82
Twists, 124, 126
Two-tone, 93, 95

V
Valrhona chocolate bars, 24
Van Damme, 14, 171, 173
Vanilla, 94, 127, 139–40
Vanilla essence, 128, 140
Variation, 20, 82, 97, 123
Vernet, 53–54, 173
Video, 1, 49, 101, 111, 143
Vienna, 14, 171
Viennoiserie, 1, 5, 10, 22, 40, 88, 105, 107, 122, 171–72
Viennoiserie candidate Peter Yuen, 44
Viennoiserie pieces bake, small, 39
Viennoiserie production, 105, 157
Volume, 16, 23, 35, 38, 40, 92, 103, 138, 145

W
Warm climate, 28, 167
Warmth, 19, 32, 34–35
Wash, 32, 76, 98
Water, 19, 22, 24–25, 27–28, 31–35, 38, 41–42, 44, 86, 90, 104–5, 157–58, 160
  filtered, 22, 32–33, 147
  warm, 18, 34–35
Water temperature, 7, 27, 33–34

Weekendbakery.com, 7, 20–21, 173
White bread flour, 21
Wholemeal, 22, 31, 41–42
Wholemeal flour, 21, 30, 32
Wiley, John, 171–73
Willan, 14, 171, 173
Wire racks, 17, 111
Wobble Test, 17, 77, 88, 172
Woodgrain Effect Croissant, 5, 104
Work, 1, 9, 12–14, 27, 37, 71, 75, 81, 119, 121, 167–68
Work surface, 63, 110
World, 9–10, 12, 18, 38, 51, 102, 157
World championships, 10, 121
World-class baker David Bedu, 81
World Silver Medal, 5, 121–22
Www.youtube.com/watch, 111, 170

Y
Yankellow, 53, 174
Yeast, 14, 18, 22–23, 29, 34, 37, 74, 77, 105, 107, 159–60
  active, 18
  commercial, 108
  instant, 18
  osmotolerant, 147
  special, 18
  wild, 30–31, 33–34
Yeast Biotechnology, 172
Yeast fermentation, 158, 160
Yeast forms, 19
Yeast reproduction, 18
Yeast's reproduction rate, 18
Yeasts Used, 3, 18
YouTube, 1–3, 49, 88, 101
YouTube Channel, 12, 111, 127, 129, 169
Youtu.be/NBm1Ti-YAWU, 129, 169

Z

Zang ,13, 170,171

Dear Reader,

I want to thank you for purchasing my book, The Art of Lamination. I hope you enjoyed the book's information and methods and that it will assist you in making great Croissants and laminated pastry. If you have any questions that you did not have answered in my book, connect and send me a message to my Instagram account. I regularly update my YouTube channel with product and techniques. Finally, I set up a FaceBook page, *The Art of Lamination*, which will regularly be updated with posts and information. I can also be contacted on this page.

Kind regards,

Jimmy Griffin.

Website: http://jimmyg.ie

YouTube: http://www.youtube.com/c/JimmyGriffinbaking/

Instagram: @jimmyg51